9th Workshop on Syntax, Semantics and Structure in Statistical Translation 2015

(SSST-9)

Held at NAACL HLT 2015

Denver, Colorado, USA
4 June 2015

Editors:

D. Wu
E. Agirre
N. Aranberri

ISBN: 978-1-5108-0430-2

Printed from e-media with permission by:

Curran Associates, Inc.
57 Morehouse Lane
Red Hook, NY 12571

Some format issues inherent in the e-media version may also appear in this print version.

Printed by Curran Associates, Inc. (2015)

Association for Computational Linguistics
209 N. Eighth Street
Stroudsburg, Pennsylvania 18360

Phone: 1-570-476-8006
Fax: 1-570-476-0860

acl@aclweb.org

Additional copies of this publication are available from:

Curran Associates, Inc.
57 Morehouse Lane
Red Hook, NY 12571 USA
Phone: 845-758-0400
Fax: 845-758-2634
Email: curran@proceedings.com
Web: www.proceedings.com

Introduction

The Ninth Workshop on Syntax, Semantics and Structure in Statistical Translation (SSST-9) was held on 4 June 2015 following the NAACL HLT 2015 conference in Denver, Colorado. Like the first eight SSST workshops in 2007, 2008, 2009, 2010, 2011, 2012, 2013 and 2014, it aimed to bring together researchers from different communities working in the rapidly growing field of structured statistical models of natural language translation.

This year's SSST featured an award for best paper to advance statistical MT using lexical semantics and deep language processing. The €500 prize was sponsored by the European Union QTLeap project (http://qtleap.eu, FP7-ICT-2013.4.1-610516), which aims to research and deliver an articulated methodology for machine translation that explores deep language engineering approaches in view of breaking the way to translations of higher quality.

We selected 13 papers and extended abstracts for this year's workshop, many of which reflect statistical machine translation's movement toward not only tree-structured and syntactic models incorporating stochastic synchronous/transduction grammars, but also increasingly semantic models and the closely linked issues of deep syntax and shallow semantics, vector space representations to support these approaches, and semantic evaluation methodologies.

Thanks are due once again to our authors and our Program Committee for making the ninth SSST workshop another success.

Dekai Wu, Marine Carpuat, Eneko Agirre and Nora Aranberri

Organizers:

Dekai Wu, Hong Kong University of Science and Technology (HKUST)
Marine Carpuat, University of Maryland
Eneko Agirre, University of the Basque Country (UPV/EHU)
Nora Aranberri, University of the Basque Country (UPV/EHU)

Program Committee:

Timothy Baldwin, University of Melbourne
Ondřej Bojar, Charles University in Prague
Aljoscha Burchardt, German Research Centre for Artificial Intelligence (DFKI)
Francisco Casacuberta, Universitat Politècnica de València
Colin Cherry, National Research Council (NRC) Canada
David Chiang, USC/ISI
Stephen Clark, University of Cambridge
Kevin Duh, Nara Institute of Science and Technology (NAIST)
Marc Dymetman, Xerox Research Centre Europe
Daniel Gildea, University of Rochester
Nal Kalchbrenner, University of Oxford
Philipp Koehn, University of Edinburgh
Gorka Labaka, University of the Basque Country (UPV/EHU)
Alon Lavie, Carnegie Mellon University
Chi-kiu Lo, Hong Kong University of Science and Technology (HKUST)
Markus Saers, Hong Kong University of Science and Technology (HKUST)
Khalil Sima'an, University of Amsterdam
Ivan Vulić, University of Leuven
Taro Watanabe, Google
Andy Way, Dublin City University
Deyi Xiong, Soochow University
François Yvon, LIMSI

Table of Contents

Conference Program

2015/06/04

08:55–09:00 ***Opening Remarks***

09:00–10:30 **Session 1**

09:00–10:00 *Invited Talk*
Philipp Koehn

10:00–10:30 *Harmonizing word alignments and syntactic structures for extracting phrasal translation equivalents*
Dun Deng, Nianwen Xue and Shiman Guo

10:30–11:00 **Coffee Break**

11:00–12:30 **Session 2**

11:00–11:30 *Non-projective Dependency-based Pre-Reordering with Recurrent Neural Network for Machine Translation*
Antonio Valerio Miceli Barone and Giuseppe Attardi

11:30–12:00 *Translating Negation: Induction, Search And Model Errors*
Federico Fancellu and Bonnie Webber

12:00–12:30 *SMT error analysis and mapping to syntactic, semantic and structural fixes*
Nora Aranberri

2015/06/04 (continued)

12:30–13:55 Lunch Break

13:55–14:30 Session 3

13:55–14:00 ***QTLeap Best Paper Award***

14:00–14:30 *Unsupervised False Friend Disambiguation Using Contextual Word Clusters and Parallel Word Alignments*
Maryam Aminian, Mahmoud Ghoneim and Mona Diab

14:30–15:30 Session 4: Posters

14:30–14:35 *METEOR-WSD: Improved Sense Matching in MT Evaluation*
Marianna Apidianaki and Benjamin Marie

14:35–14:40 *Analyzing English-Spanish Named-Entity enhanced Machine Translation*
Mikel Artetxe, Eneko Agirre, Iñaki Alegria and Gorka Labaka

14:40–14:45 *Predicting Prepositions for SMT*
Marion Weller, Alexander Fraser and Sabine Schulte im Walde

14:45–14:50 *Translation reranking using source phrase dependency features*
Antonio Valerio Miceli Barone

14:50–14:55 *Semantics-based pretranslation for SMT using fuzzy matches*
Tom Vanallemeersch and Vincent Vandeghinste

2015/06/04 (continued)

15:30–16:00 Coffee Break

16:00–17:00 Session 5

16:00–16:30 *What Matters Most in Morphologically Segmented SMT Models?*
Mohammad Salameh, Colin Cherry and Grzegorz Kondrak

16:30–17:00 *Improving Chinese-English PropBank Alignment*
Shumin Wu and Martha Palmer

Harmonizing word alignments and syntactic structures for extracting phrasal translation equivalents

Dun Deng, Nianwen Xue and Shiman Guo
Computer Science Department
Brandeis University
415 South Street, Waltham, MA 02453
ddeng@brandeis.edu, xuen@brandeis.edu, shim@brandeis.edu

Abstract

Accurate identification of phrasal translation equivalents is critical to both phrase-based and syntax-based machine translation systems. We show that the extraction of many phrasal translation equivalents is made impossible by word alignments done without taking syntactic structures into consideration. To address the problem, we propose a new annotation scheme where word alignment and the alignment of non-terminal nodes (i.e., phrases) are done simultaneously to avoid conflicts between word alignments and syntactic structures. Relying on this new alignment approach, we construct a Hierarchically Aligned Chinese-English Parallel Treebank (HACEPT), and show that all phrasal translation equivalents can be automatically extracted based on the phrase alignments in HACEPT.

1 Introduction

During the past two decades since the emergence of the statistical paradigm of Machine Translation (MT) (Brown et al., 1993), the field of Statistical Machine Translation (SMT) has attained consensus on the need for structural mappings between languages in MT. Accurately identifying structural mappings (i.e., phrasal translation equivalents) is critical to the performance of both phrase-based systems (Koehn, Och, and Marcu, 2003; Och and Ney, 2004) and syntax-based systems (Chiang, 2005; Chiang, 2007; Galley et al., 2004). The fact is that phrasal translation equivalents are identified based on word alignments, so how word alignments are done directly affects the identification of phrasal translation equivalents. As reported by (Zhu, Li, and Xiao, 2015), even one spurious word alignment can prevent some desirable phrasal translation equivalents from being extracted. The unfortunate fact is that spurious word alignments abound in current word-aligned parallel texts used for extracting phrasal translation equivalents. This is because the word alignments in these parallel texts, whether they are induced in an unsupervised manner such as that described by (Och and Ney, 2003) or manually annotated based on existing word alignment standards such as (Li, Ge, and Strassel, 2009) and (Melamed, 1998), are generally done as an independent task without taking syntactic structures into consideration. As a result, conflicts between word alignments and syntactic structures are inevitable, and when such a conflict arises, the extraction of desirable phrasal translation equivalents will be impossible.

To address this shortcoming, we designed a hierarchical alignment scheme in which word-level alignment (namely alignment of terminal nodes) and phrase-level alignments (namely alignment of non-terminals) are done simultaneously in a coordinated manner so that conflicts between word alignments and syntactic structures are avoided. Based on this alignment scheme, we constructed a Hierarchically Aligned Chinese-English Parallel Treebank (HACEPT) which currently has 9,897 sentence pairs. We show that this hierarchically aligned corpus provides a new way to extract hierarchical translation rules and can be used as a training corpus to learn this type of alignments.

The rest of the paper is organized like this: Section shows how phrasal translation equivalents can be

Proceedings of SSST-9, Ninth Workshop on Syntax, Semantics and Structure in Statistical Translation, pages 1–9,
Denver, Colorado, June 4, 2015.

made impossible to extract by word alignments done without considering syntactic structures. To avoid the problem, Section 3 introduces our new alignment scheme and how HACEPT is constructed using the scheme. Section 4 shows how hierarchical translation rules can be extracted from the phrase alignments in HACEPT. We also provide statistics about two important aspects of the rules, namely the distributions of terminal and non-terminal nodes in the rules and the number of terminal nodes contained in a single rule. Section 5 discusses some work in the literature that are related to what is discussed in this paper. Section 6 concludes the paper and points out furture work to do.

2 Spurious word alignments impede the extraction of phrase pairs

Spurious word alignments arise in any word alignment practice where the alignment is done as an independent task without taking sysntactic structures into consideration, regardless of whether the alignment is automatically generated by utilizing a word aligner such as the GIZA++ toolkit (Och and Ney, 2003) or manually annotated using alignment standards such as (Li, Ge, and Strassel, 2009) and (Melamed, 1998). (Zhu, Li, and Xiao, 2015) has described how a spurious word alignment in automatically generated word alignments prevents some phrasal translation equivalents from being extracted. In this section, we will show how spurious word alignments in human annotated word alignments make the extraction of phrasal translation equivalents impossible.

Consider the following example quoted from (Li, Ge, and Strassel, 2009), where the relevant word alignment in each sentence/phrase pair is highlighted by underlining. Note that the word alignments are done without taking syntactic structures into consideration, as can be told from the fact that all the underlined aligned multi-word strings do not correspond to a constituent in a Penn TreeBank (Marcus, Santorini, and Marcinkiewicz, 1993) or Chinese TreeBank (Xue et al., 2005) parse tree.

1a. He is visiting Beijing <> 他 正 访问 北京

1b. He has gone to Beijing <> 他 去 北京 了

1c. to quickly and efficiently solve the problem <> 迅速 有效地 解决 问题

1d. Results can be obtained by doing experiments <> 做 实验 可以 得出 结果

1e. We fully agree with the Chinese position that there is only one China in the world <> 我们 完全 同意 中方 的 立场，世界 上 只 有 一 个 中国

Just like the spurious word alignment discussed by (Zhu, Li, and Xiao, 2015), the underlined word alignment in each of the sentence/phrase pair above makes it impossible to extract at least one diserable phrasal translation equivalent. For each of the sentence/phrase pair in (1), (2) lists the phrasal translation equivalents that cannot be extracted due to the word alignment done in that pair:

2a. visiting Beijing <> 访问 北京

2b. gone to Beijing <> 去 北京

2c. solve the problem <> 解决 问题

2d. doing experiments <> 做 实验

2e. the Chinese position <> 中方 的 立场

The reason why the phrasal translation equivalents in (2) cannot be extracted is because a word in a phrase on one side is aligned to a word that is not part of the corresponding phrase on the other side. Take (2c) for instance. The Chinese verb 解决/solve in the phrase 解决 问题 is aligned to both *solve* and *to* in (1c), which is not part of the phrase *solve the problem*. As a result, the phrase pair in (2c) cannot be obtained.

It is not desirable that legitimate phrase pairs such as those in (2) cannot be extracted. To fix the problem, Section 3 proposes a new alignment scheme.

3 Hierarchical alignment and the creation of HACEPT

Hierarchical alignment is a new alignment scheme where both terminal nodes (words) and non-terminal nodes (linguistic phrases) between parallel parse trees are aligned in a coordinated way so that conflicts in the form of redundancies and incompatabilities between word alignments and syntatic structures are avoided. We use this scheme to construct HACEPT with the goal of providing the field of MT with a resource that has human annotated tree-structured mappings for MT training purposes.

The word alignment done in HACEPT differs from the common practice of word alignment in the field (Melamed, 1998; Li, Ge, and Strassel, 2009) in that the requirement that every word in a sentence pair needs to be word-aligned is relaxed. On the word level, we only align words that have an equivalent in terms of lexical meaning and grammatical function. For those words that do not have a translation counterpart, we leave them unaligned at word level and instead the appropriate phrases in which they appear. This strategy makes sure that both redundancies and incompatibilities between word alignments and syntactic structures are avoided. In addition, artificial ambiguities are also eliminated. These points will be illustrated in the discussion of the concrete example in Figure 1 below.

We take the Chinese-English portion of the Parallel Aligned Treebank (PAT) described in (Li et al., 2012) for annotation. Our data have three batches: one batch is weblogs, one batch is postings from online discussion forums and one batch is news wire. The English sentences in the data set are annotated based on the original Penn TreeBank (PTB) annotation stylebook (Bies et al., 1995) as well as its extensions (Warner et al., 2004), while the Chinese sentences in the data set are annotated based on the Chinese TreeBank (CTB) annotation guidelines (Xue and Xia, 1998) and its extensions ZhangandXue12. The PAT has no phrase alignments and the word alignments in it are done under the requirement that all the words in a sentence should be aligned.

Next we discuss our annotation procedure in detail. Our annotators are presented with sentence pairs that come with parallel parse trees. The task of the annotator is to decide, first on the word level and then on the phrase level, if a word or phrase needs to be aligned at all, and if so, to which word or phrase it should be aligned. The decisions about word alignment and phrase alignment are not independent, and must obey well-formedness constraints as outlined in (Tinsley et al., 2007):

a. A non-terminal node can only be aligned once.

b. if Node n_c is aligned to Node n_e, then the descendants of n_c can only be aligned to descendants of n_e.

c. if Node n_c is aligned to Node n_e, then the ancestors of n_c can only be aligned to ancestors of n_e.

This means that once a word alignment is in place, it puts constraints on phrase alignments. A pair of non-terminal nodes (n_c, n_e) cannot be aligned if a word that is a descendant of n_c is aligned to a word that is not a descendant of n_e on the word level.

Let us use the concrete example in Figure 1 to illustrate the annotation process, which is guided by a set of detailed annotation guidelines. On the word level, only those words that are connected with a dashed line are aligned since they have equivalents. Note that the Chinese prenominal modification marker 的 and the existential verb 有/have, and the English determiner *the*, the relative pronoun *who*, the preposition *of*, the expletive subject *it*, the copular verb *is*, the infinitive marker *to* and the conjunction word *both* are all left unaligned on the word level. Aligning these words will generate artificial ambiguous cases and create both redundancies and incompatibilities between word alignments and parse trees.

For instance, if 的 is to be word-aligned, it could be glued to the preceding verb 喋喋不休 and the whole string will be aligned to *harp*. Note that 喋喋不休 and *harp* are both unambiguous and form a one-to-one correspondence. With the word alignment between 喋喋不休 的 and *harp*, we make the unambiguous *harp* correspond to both 喋喋不休 and 喋喋不休 的 (and possibly more strings), thus creating a spurious ambiguity. Also note that the string 喋喋不休 的 does not form a constituent in the Chinese parse tree, so the word alignment is incompatible with the syntactic structure of the sentence. By leaving 的 unaligned, we avoid both the spurious ambiguity and the incompatibility.

As for redundancies, consider the English determiner *the*, which has no translation counterpart in the Chinese sentence. If *the* is to be word-aligned, it could be attached to the noun *people* and the whole string *the people* will be aligned to 人们. This will create a redundancy, since the English parse tree already groups *the* and *people* together to form an NP, and therefore there is no need to repeat this information on the word level by attaching *the* to *people*, especially when the word alignment also generates a spurious ambiguity for 人们, which unambiguously means *people* but is aligned to *the people*.

With word alignments in place, next the annotator needs to perform phrase alignments. Note that word alignments place restrictions on phrase alignments. For instance, VP_{c0} cannot be a possible alignment for VP_{e1}, because 通常, a descendant of VP_{c0}, is aligned to *often*, which is not a descendant of VP_{e1}. For a phrase that does have a possible alignment, the annotator needs to decide whether the possible phrase alignment can be actually made. This is a challenging task since, for a given phrase, there usually are more than one candidate from which a single alignment needs to be picked. For instance, for the English ADJP, there are in total two possible phrase alignments, namely VP_{c6}, and VP_{c7}, both of which obey the well-formedness constraints. Since a non-terminal node is not allowed to be aligned to multiple non-terminal nodes on the other side, the annotator needs to choose one among all the candidates. This highlights the point that the alignment of non-terminal nodes cannot be deterministically inferred from the alignment of terminal nodes. This is especially true given our approach where some terminal nodes are left unaligned on the word level. For instance, the reason why VP_{c7} is a possible alignment for ADJP is because the word 有 is left unaligned. If 有 were aligned with, say, *is*, VP_{c7} could not be aligned with ADJP since *is* is not a descendant of ADJP and aligning the two nodes will violate Constraint *b*.

While Constraints *b* and *c* can be enforced automatically given the word alignments, the decisions regarding the alignment of non-terminal nodes which satisfy Constraint *a* are based on linguistic considerations. One key consideration is to determine which non-terminal nodes encapsulate the grammatical relations signaled by the unaligned words so that the alignment of the non-terminal nodes will effectively capture the unaligned words in their syntactic context. When identifying non-terminal nodes to align, we follow two seemingly conflicting general principles:

- Phrase alignment should not sever key dependencies involving the grammatical relation signaled by an unaligned word.
- Phrase alignment should be minimal, in the sense that the phrase alignment should contain only the elements involved in the grammatical relation, and nothing more.

The first principle ensures that the grammatical relation is properly encapsulated in the aligned non-terminal nodes. For example in Figure 1, if we attach the English preposition *on* to *tolls* and aligning them to 通行费, we would fail to capture the lexical dependency between *harp* and *on*. Aligning VP_{c2} with VP_{e2} captures the dependency.

The first principle in and of itself is insufficient to produce desired alignment. Taken to the extreme, it can be trivially satisfied by aligning the two root nodes of the sentence pair. We also need the alignment to be minimal, in the sense that aligned non-terminal nodes should contain only the elements involved in the grammatical relation, and nothing more. These two requirements used in conjunction ensure that a unique phrase alignment can be found for each unaligned word. The phrase alignments in Figure 1 which are indicated by blue dotted lines, all satisfy these two principles.

Following the principles and the procedure introduced above, we constructued HACEPT,[1] which has 9,897 sentence pairs. In the next section, we show how the alignments in HACEPT can help to extract translation rules.

4 Extracting hierarchical translation rules in HACEPT

Hierarchical translation rules can be automatically extracted from the phrase alignments in HACEPT. Take a pair of aligned non-terminal nodes (n_c, n_e), a translation rule based on the alignment between n_c and n_e can be extracted like this: Check each of the immediate daughter nodes of both n_c and n_e. For any of the daughter nodes that is aligned, stop looking down into the node and keep the phrase category label of the node as a variable the rule. For each daughter node that is not aligned, recursively traverse its children until either an aligned node is found, in which case its phrase category label will be kept as a variable in the rule, or a terminal node is

[1] As of the writing of this paper, we are in the process of doing adjudication on the double annotation done to create HACEPT. We look forward to finishing adjudication soon and releasing the resouce to the public.

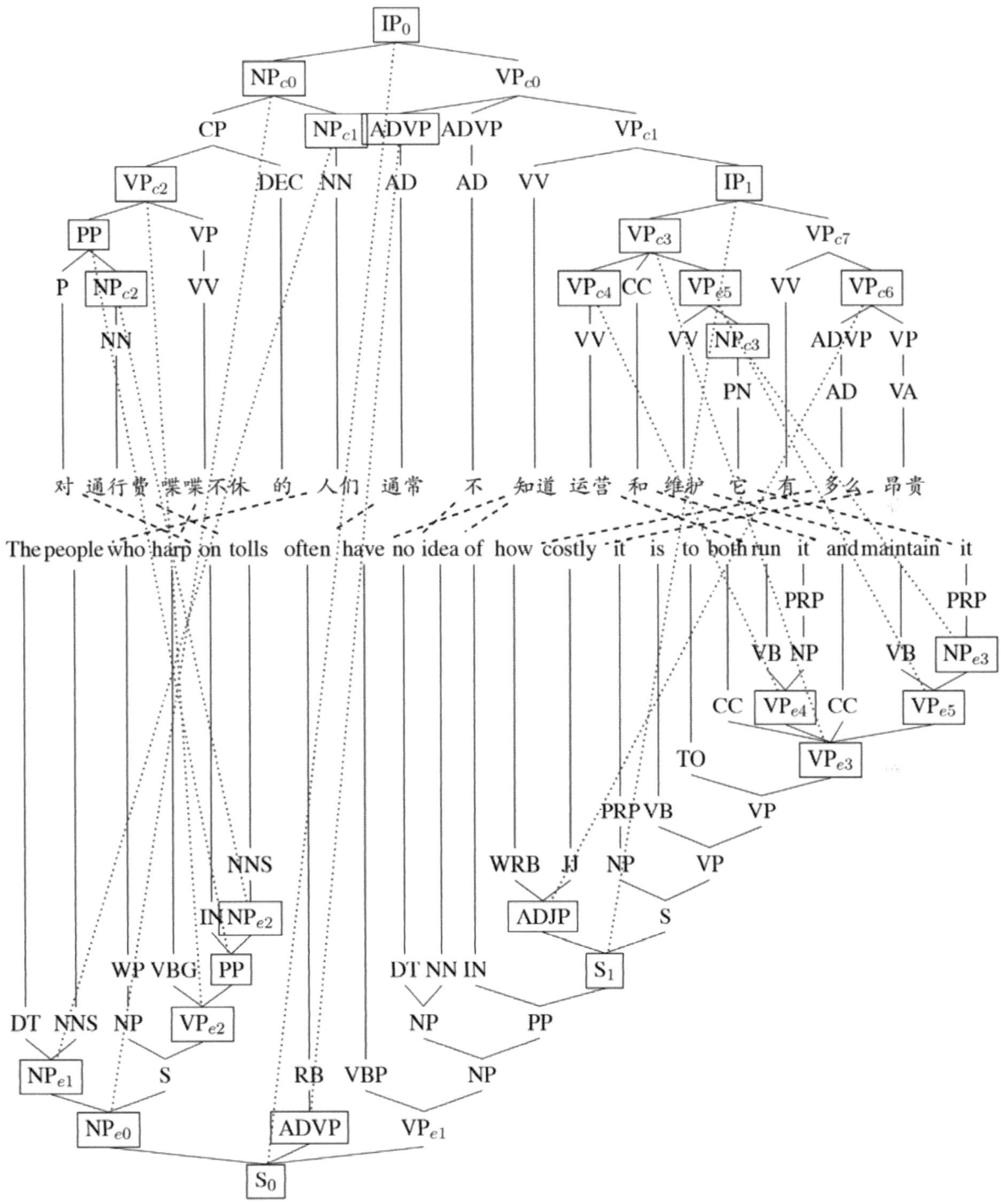

Figure 1: A hierarchically aligned sentence pair

reached, in which case the word is included as part of the translation rule.

To illustrate the rule extraction process specified above, let us take the phrase alignment between NP_{c0} and NP_{e0} in Figure 1 for instance. The search starts top-down from the two root nodes. On the Chinese side, NP_{c0} has two immediate daughter nodes: CP and NP_{c1}. NP_{c1} is aligned, so we stop looking inside the node and just keep the phrase category label of the node as part of the rule. CP is not aligned, so we keep checking its two immediate daughter nodes: VP_{c2} and DEC. VP_{c2} is aligned and will not be further checked. DEC is not aligned and dominates the terminal node 的, which will be kept in the rule. Since DEC is the last node inside NP_{c0} and a terminal node is reached, the search on the Chinese side ends. The same procedure will simultaneously take place on the English side, and when the search is done, we will get the translation rule in (3) below:

(3) $NP_{c0} \Leftrightarrow NP_{e0}$:

VP_{c2} 的 NP_{c1} <> NP_{e1} who VP_{e2}

Note that the rule contains both terminals (的 and *who*) and non-terminals represented by phrase category labels.

The rule in (3) illustrates one type of rule, namely the rules containing both terminal and non-terminal nodes. There are also rules with only terminal nodes and rules with only non-terminal nodes. Figure 1 has quite a few examples for the former and an example is given below:

(4) $NP_{c2} \Leftrightarrow NP_{e2}$:

通行费 <> tolls

The rule above contains only terminals. Figure 1 does not contain an example for rules with only non-terminals, but such rules do exist and here is a common example:

(5) IP $\Leftrightarrow$ S:

NP_{subj} VP_{pred} <> NP_{subj} VP_{pred}

The rule above illustrates parallel sentences whose subjects and predicates are both aligned.

Table 1 provides the statistics of the distribution of the three types of rules in HACEPT.

Rule types	No.	Percentage
with only terminals	52379	50.46
with only non-terminals	2621	2.53
with both	48796	47.01
Total	103796	100

Table 1: Rule distribution

Given the importance of hierarchical translation rules for MT, a natural question to ask about the hierarchical translation rules extracted from HACEPT is this: are these rules usable? The most crucial factor deciding the usability of a rule is its length in terms of the number of terminal nodes it contains. If a rule contains too many terminal nodes, it cannot be easily used for MT purposes. Table 2 provides the statistics about the number of terminal node (TN) in the extracted rules:

TN	Rule	Percentage	Cumulative
0	6974	6.72	6.72
1	4017	3.87	10.59
2	30829	29.70	40.29
3	18780	17.09	58.38
4	12897	12.43	70.81
5	9387	9.04	79.85
6	6079	5.86	85.71
7	4404	4.24	89.95
More than 7	10429	10.05	1

Table 2: Rule length

As shown by the table, 89.95 percent of the rules contain 7 or less than 7 terminal nodes. There are still 10 percent of the rules that contain more than 7 terminal nodes.

One primary reason that increases the number of terminal nodes in a rule is how the parse trees are designed. To be specific, some parts of the parse trees are designed to be flat, presumably for the sake of increasing treebank annotation throughput, but this makes some otherwise legitimate phrase alignments inaccessible unless we change the underlying parse trees. When a phrase alignment cannot be made, some terminal nodes will be left out to appear in the rule. This is illustrated by Figure 1.

On the Chinese side, there is a node, namely VP_{c0}, which dominates the predicate part of the sentence.

On the English side, the predicate part of the English sentence is split into ADVP and VP_{e1}, and there is no single node dominating these two nodes. As a result, VP_{c0} has no phrase alignment. Suppose a node VP_{e0} is created that includes ADVP and VP_{e1} as its immediate daughters, VP_{c0} and VP_{e0} could be aligned. (7) below is the rule based on the alignment between the two sentences in Figure 1, and (8) is the rule based on the alignment between the two sentences if a node is created for the predicate of the English sentence and aligned to VP_{c0}.

(6) $IP_0 \Leftrightarrow S_0$

NP_{c0} ADVP 不知道 IP_1 <> NP_{e0} ADVP have no idea of S_1

(7) $IP_0 \Leftrightarrow S_0$

NP_{c0} VP_{c0} <> NP_{e0} VP_{e0}

($VP_{e0} \Rightarrow$ ADVP VP_{e1})

Note that the rule in (6) has 6 terminal nodes in total whereas the rule in (7) has none. This is a good example to illustrate the fact that a flat structure makes some legitimate phrase alignment impossible and as a result increases the number of terminal nodes in a rule.

There is another place in Figure 1 that has the same problem. Note that the Chinese VP_{c0} has three immediate daughter nodes: ADVP, ADVP, and VP_{c1}. This structure is flat and can become deeper if an intermediate node is created to dominate the second ADVP and VP_{c1}. This node can then combine with the first ADVP to form VP_{c0}. Note that this intermediate node will serve as the phrase alignment of VP_{e1}, which cannot be unaligned in the figure. With the phrase alignment between VP_{e1} and the hypothetical intermediate node (call it VP_{c9}), the number of terminal nodes in (6) will be reduced to zero even without the creation of VP_{e0} in (7). The new rule looks like this:

(8) $IP_0 \Leftrightarrow S_0$

NP_{c0} ADVP VP_{c9} <> NP_{e0} ADVP VP_{e1}

($VP_{c9} \Rightarrow$ ADVP VP_{c1})

In the near future, we plan to binarize the flat structures as illustrated above to create some intermediate nodes, which can be aligned and reduce the number of terminal nodes in existing rules.

5 Related work

To address the problem caused by spurious word alignments, there has been research done to improve word alignment quality by incorporating syntactic information into word alignments (May and Knight, 2007; Fossum, Knight, and Abney, 2008). Another research direction has been explored to conduct syntactic alignment between parse trees (Tinsley et al., 2007; Pauls et al., 2010; Sun, Zhang, and Tan, 2010b; Sun, Zhang, and Tan, 2010a), and implements syntactic rule extraction based on syntactic alignment instead of word alignment. Our work reported in Section 3 can be viewed as a combination of these two lines of research.

There has also been reasearch done to automatically obtain phrasal translation equivalents (Ambati and Lavie, 2008; Hanneman, Burroughs, and Lavie, 2011; Lavie, Parlikar, and Ambati, 2008; Zhu, Li, and Xiao, 2015). This line of research is different from our work in two respects:

First, word alignment as the foundation of phrase-pair extraction is done differently in the two approaches. Automatic extraction of phrase pairs uses automatically generated word alignments, where there are lots of spurious word alignments, which, as pointed out by (Zhu, Li, and Xiao, 2015), are harmful to rule extraction and affect translation quality. By contrast, HACEPT is free of spurious word alignments. As already mentioned in Section 3, all the word alignments in HACEPT are compatible with the syntactic structures and will not block any legitimate phrase alignment.

Second, phrase alignment is inferred from word alignment in automatic approaches. As reported by (Ambati and Lavie, 2008), in places where language-particular function words such as English auxiliary verbs that exist in one language but not the other are involved, there are usually more than one candiate in the language that has the function words for a phrase in the language that does not have a counterpart of the function words. Automatic inference cannot always make the right decision in such situations. We have strict standards for choosing the correct phrase alignment in such cases and as a result, HACEPT can function as a training corpus for automatic approaches.

6 Conclusion

In this paper, we report a resource we have constructed with a novel alignment scheme. The corpus contains both word and phrase alignments and can help extract hierarchical translation rules and train syntax-based MT models. The next step is, of course, to do MT experiments with this resource to see if it indeed helps to improve system performance.

Acknowledgments

This work is supported by the IBM subcontract No. 4913014934 under DARPA Prime Contract No. 0011-12-C-0015 entitled "Broad Operational Language Translation". We would like to thank Libin Shen and Salim Roukos for their inspiration and discussion during early stages of the project, Abe Ittycheriah and Niyu Ge for their help with setting up the data, Loretta Bandera for developing and maintaining the annotation tool, and two anonymous reviewers for their helpful comments. We are grateful for the hard work of our annotators Hui Gao, Tseming Wang and Lingya Zhou. Any opinions, findings, conclusions or recommendations expressed in this material are those of the authors and do not necessarily reflect those of the sponsor or any of the people mentioned above.

References

Ambati, Vamshi and Alon Lavie. 2008. Improving syntax driven translation models by re-structuring divergent and non-isomorphic parse tree structures. In *Proceedings of AMTA-2008 Student Research Workshop*, pages 235--244.

Bies, Ann, Mark Ferguson, Karen Katz, Robert MacIntyre, Victoria Tredinnick, Grace Kim, Mary Ann Marcinkiewicz, and Britta Schasberger. 1995. Bracketing guidelines for treebank ii style penn treebank project. Technical report, University of Pennsylvania.

Brown, Peter F., Vincent J. Della Pietra, Stephen A. Della Pietra, and Robert L. Mercer. 1993. The mathematics of statistical machine translation: Parameter estimation. *Computational Linguistics*, 19(2):263--311.

Chiang, David. 2005. A hierarchical phrase-based model for statistical machine translation. In *Proceedings of the 43rd Annual Meeting of the Association for Computational Linguistics*, pages 263--270. Association for Computational Linguistics.

Chiang, David. 2007. Hierarchical phrase-based translation. *Computational Linguistics*, 33(2):201--228.

Fang, Licheng and Chengqing Zong. 2008. An efficient approach to rule redundancy reduction in hierarchical phrase-based translation. In *Proceedings of NLP-KE '08 International Conference on Natural Language Processing and Knowledge Engineering*, pages 1--6.

Fossum, V., K. Knight, and S. Abney. 2008. Using syntax to improve word alignment precision for syntax-based machine translation. In *Proceedings of the Third Workshop on Statistical Machine Translation*, pages 44--52.

Galley, Michel, Mark Hopkins, Kevin Knight, and Daniel Marcu. 2004. What's in a translation rule? In Susan Dumais, Daniel Marcu, and Salim Roukos, editors, *HLT-NAACL 2004: Main Proceedings*, pages 273--280.

Hanneman, Greg, Michelle Burroughs, and Alon Lavie. 2011. A general-purpose rule extractor for scfg-based machine translation. In *Proceedings of SSST-5, Fifth Workshop on Syntax, Semantics and Structure in Statistical Translation*, pages 135--144.

Koehn, Philipp, Franz Josef Och, and Daniel Marcu. 2003. Statistical phrase-based translation. In *Proceedings of the 2003 Conference of the North American Chapter of the Association for Computational Linguistics on Human Language Technology*, volume 1, pages 48--54.

Lavie, Alon, Alok Parlikar, and Vamshi Ambati. 2008. Syntax-driven learning of sub-sentential translation equivalents and translation rules from parsed parallel corpora. In *Proceedings of the Second ACL Workshop on Syntax and Structure in Statistical Translation (SSST-2)*, pages 87--95.

Li, Xuansong, Niyu Ge, and Stephanie Strassel. 2009. Tagging guidelines for chinese-english word alignment. Technical report, Linguistic Data Consortium.

Li, Xuansong, Stephanie Strassel, Stephen Grimes, Safa Ismael, Mohamed Maamouri, Ann Bies, and Nianwen Xue. 2012. Parallel aligned treebanks at ldc: New challenges interfacing existing infrastructures. In *Proceedings of LREC-2012*, Istanbul, Turkey.

Marcus, Mitchell P., Beatrice Santorini, and Mary Ann Marcinkiewicz. 1993. Building a large annotated corpus of english: The penn treebank. *Computational Linguistics*, 19(2):313--330.

May, J. and K. Knight. 2007. Syntactic re-alignment models for machine translation. In *Proceedings of the*

2007 Joint Conference on Empirical Methods in Natural Language Processing and Computational Natural Language Learning (EMNLP--CoNLL), pages 360--68.

Melamed, I. Dan. 1998. Annotation style guide for the blinker project. Technical report, University of Pennsylvania.

Och, Franz Josef and Hermann Ney. 2003. A systematic comparison of various statistical alignment models. *Computational Linguistics*, 29(1):19--51.

Och, Franz Josef and Hermann Ney. 2004. The alignment template approach to statistical machine translation. *Computational Linguistics*, 30(4):417--449.

Pauls, A., D. Klein, D. Chiang, and K. Knight. 2010. Unsupervised syntactic alignment with inversion transduction grammars. In *Proceedings of Human Language Technologies: The 2010 Annual Conference of the North American Chapter of the Association for Computational Linguistics (HLT--NAACL)*, pages 118--26.

Sun, J., M. Zhang, and C.L. Tan. 2010a. Discriminative induction of sub-tree alignment using limited labeled data. In *Proceedings of the 23rd International Conference on Computational Linguistics (COLING)*, pages 1047--55.

Sun, J., M. Zhang, and C.L. Tan. 2010b. Exploring syntactic structural features for sub-tree alignment using bilingual tree kernels. In *Proceedings of the 48th Annual Meeting of the Association for Computational Linguistics (ACL)*, pages 306--15.

Tinsley, John, Ventsislav Zhechev, Mary Hearne, and Andy Way. 2007. Robust language pair-independent subtree alignment. In *Proceedings of Machine Translation Summit XI*, Copenhagen, Denmark.

Warner, Colin, Ann Bies, Christine Brisson, and Justin Mott. 2004. Addendum to the penn treebank ii style bracketing guidelines: Biomedical treebank annotation. Technical report, University of Pennsylvania.

Xue, Nianwen and Fei Xia. 1998. The bracketing guidelines for penn chinese treebank project. Technical report, University of Pennsylvania.

Xue, Nianwen, Fei Xia, Fudong Chiou, and Martha Palmer. 2005. The penn chinese treebank: Phrase structure annotation of a large corpus. *Natural Language Engineering*, 11(2):207--238.

Zhu, Jingbo, Qiang Li, and Tong Xiao. 2015. Improving syntactic rule extraction through deleting spurious links with translation span alignment. *Natural Language Engineering*, pages 1--23.

Non-projective Dependency-based Pre-Reordering with Recurrent Neural Network for Machine Translation

Antonio Valerio Miceli-Barone
Università di Pisa
Largo B. Pontecorvo, 3
56127 Pisa, Italy
miceli@di.unipi.it

Giuseppe Attardi
Università di Pisa
Largo B. Pontecorvo, 3
56127 Pisa, Italy
attardi@di.unipi.it

Abstract

The quality of statistical machine translation performed with phrase based approaches can be increased by permuting the words in the source sentences in an order which resembles that of the target language. We propose a class of recurrent neural models which exploit source-side dependency syntax features to reorder the words into a target-like order. We evaluate these models on the German-to-English language pair, showing significant improvements over a phrase-based Moses baseline, obtaining a quality similar or superior to that of hand-coded syntactical reordering rules.

1 Introduction

Statistical machine translation is typically performed using phrase-based systems (Koehn et al., 2007). These systems can usually produce accurate local reordering but they have difficulties dealing with the long-distance reordering that tends to occur between certain language pairs (Birch et al., 2008).

The quality of phrase-based machine translation can be improved by reordering the words in each sentence of source-side of the parallel training corpus in a "target-like" order and then applying the same transformation as a pre-processing step to input strings during execution.

When the source-side sentences can be accurately parsed, pre-reordering can be performed using hand-coded rules. This approach has been successfully applied to German-to-English (Collins et al., 2005) and other languages. The main issue with it is that these rules must be designed for each specific language pair, which requires considerable linguistic expertise.

Fully statistical approaches, on the other hand, learn the reordering relation from word alignments. Some of them learn reordering rules on the constituency (Dyer and Resnik, 2010) (Khalilov and Fonollosa, 2011) or projective dependency (Genzel, 2010), (Lerner and Petrov, 2013) parse trees of source sentences. The permutations that these methods can learn can be generally non-local (i.e. high distance) on the sentences but local (parent-child or sibling-sibling swaps) on the parse trees. Moreover, constituency or projective dependency trees may not be the ideal way of representing the syntax of non-analytic languages, which could be better described using non-projective dependency trees (Bosco and Lombardo, 2004). Other methods, based on recasting reordering as a combinatorial optimization problem (Tromble and Eisner, 2009), (Visweswariah et al., 2011), can learn to generate in principle arbitrary permutations, but they can only make use of minimal syntactic information (part-of-speech tags) and therefore can't exploit the potentially valuable structural syntactic information provided by a parser.

In this work we propose a class of reordering models which attempt to close this gap by exploiting rich dependency syntax features and

Proceedings of SSST-9, Ninth Workshop on Syntax, Semantics and Structure in Statistical Translation, pages 10–20,
Denver, Colorado, June 4, 2015.

at the same time being able to process non-projective dependency parse trees and generate permutations which may be non-local both on the sentences and on the parse trees.
We represent these problems as sequence prediction machine learning tasks, which we address using recurrent neural networks.

We applied our model to reorder German sentences into an English-like word order as a pre-processing step for phrase-based machine translation, obtaining significant improvements over the unreordered baseline system and quality comparable to the hand-coded rules introduced by Collins et al. (2005).

2 Reordering as a walk on a dependency tree

In order to describe the non-local reordering phenomena that can occur between language pairs such as German-to-English, we introduce a reordering framework similar to (Miceli Barone and Attardi, 2013), based on a *graph walk* of the dependency parse tree of the source sentence. This framework doesn't restrict the parse tree to be projective, and allows the generation of arbitrary permutations.

Let $f \equiv (f_1, f_2, \ldots, f_{L_f})$ be a source sentence, annotated by a rooted dependency parse tree: $\forall j \in 1, \ldots, L_f, h_j \equiv PARENT(j)$

We define a *walker* process that walks from word to word across the edges of the parse tree, and at each steps optionally *emits* the current word, with the constraint that each word must be eventually emitted exactly once.
Therefore, the final string of emitted words f' is a permutation of the original sentence f, and any permutation can be generated by a suitable walk on the parse tree.

2.1 Reordering automaton

We formalize the walker process as a non-deterministic finite-state automaton.
The state v of the automaton is the tuple $v \equiv (j, E, a)$ where $j \in 1, \ldots, L_f$ is the current vertex (word index), E is the set of emitted vertices, a is the last action taken by the automaton.
The initial state is: $v(0) \equiv (root_f, \{\}, null)$ where $root_f$ is the root vertex of the parse tree.

At each step t, the automaton chooses one of the following actions:

- $EMIT$: emit the word f_j at the current vertex j. This action is enabled only if the current vertex has not been already emitted:

$$\frac{j \notin E}{(j, E, a) \overset{EMIT}{\rightarrow} (j, E \cup \{j\}, EMIT)} \quad (1)$$

- UP: move to the parent of the current vertex. Enabled if there is a parent and we did not just come down from it:

$$\frac{h_j \neq null, a \neq DOWN_j}{(j, E, a) \overset{UP}{\rightarrow} (h_j, E, UP_j)} \quad (2)$$

- $DOWN_{j'}$: move to the child j' of the current vertex. Enabled if the subtree $s(j')$ rooted at j' contains vertices that have not been already emitted and if we did not just come up from it:

$$\frac{h_{j'} = j, a \neq UP_{j'}, \exists k \in s(j') : k \notin E}{(j, E, a) \overset{DOWN_{j'}}{\rightarrow} (j', E, DOWN_{j'})} \quad (3)$$

The execution continues until all the vertices have been emitted.

We define the sequence of states of the walker automaton during one run as an *execution* $\bar{v} \in GEN(f)$. An execution also uniquely specifies the sequence of actions performed by the automation.

The preconditions make sure that all execution of the automaton always end generating a permutation of the source sentence. Furthermore, no cycles are possible: progress is made at every step, and it is not possible to enter in an execution that later turns out to be invalid.
Every permutation of the source sentence can be generated by some execution. In fact, each permutation f' can be generated by exactly one execution, which we denote as $\bar{v}(f')$.

We can split the execution $\bar{v}(f')$ into a sequence of L_f *emission fragments* $\bar{v}_j(f')$, each ending with an $EMIT$ action.
The first fragment has zero or more $DOWN_*$ actions followed by one $EMIT$ action, while each

other fragment has a non-empty sequence of UP and $DOWN_*$ actions (always zero or more UPs followed by zero or more DOWNs) followed by one $EMIT$ action.

Finally, we define an action in an execution as *forced* if it was the only action enabled at the step where it occurred.

2.2 Application

Suppose we perform reordering using a typical syntax-based system which processes source-side projective dependency parse trees and is limited to swaps between pair of vertices which are either in a parent-child relation or in a sibling relation. In such execution the UP actions are always forced, since the "walker" process never leaves a subtree before all its vertices have been emitted.

Suppose instead that we could perform reordering according to an "oracle". The executions of our automaton corresponding to these permutations will in general contain *unforced* UP actions. We define these actions, and the execution fragments that exhibit them, as *non-tree-local*.

In practice we don't have access to a reordering "oracle", but for sentences pairs in a parallel corpus we can compute heuristic "pseudo-oracle" reference permutations of the source sentences from word-alignments.

Following (Al-Onaizan and Papineni, 2006), (Tromble and Eisner, 2009), (Visweswariah et al., 2011), (Navratil et al., 2012), we generate word alignments in both the source-to-target and the target-to-source directions using IBM model 4 as implemented in GIZA++ (Och et al., 1999) and then we combine them into a symmetrical word alignment using the "grow-diag-final-and" heuristic implemented in Moses (Koehn et al., 2007).

Given the symmetric word-aligned corpus, we assign to each source-side word an integer index corresponding to the position of the leftmost target-side word it is aligned to (attaching unaligned words to the following aligned word) and finally we perform a stable sort of source-side words according to this index.

2.3 Reordering example

Consider the segment of a German sentence shown in fig. 1. The English-reordered segment "**die Währungsreserven anfangs lediglich dienen sollten zur Verteidigung**" corresponds to the English: "**the reserve assets were originally intended to provide protection**".

In order to compose this segment from the original German, the reordering automaton described in our framework must perform a complex sequence of moves on the parse tree:

- Starting from "**sollten**", descend to "**dienen**", descent to "**Währungsreserven**" and finally to "**die**". Emit it, then go up to "**Währungsreserven**", emit it and go up to "**dienen**" and up again to "**sollten**". Note that the last UP is *unforced* since "**dienen**" has not been emitted at that point and has also unemitted children. This unforced action indicates non-tree-local reordering.

- Go down to "**anfangs**". Note that the in the parse tree edge crosses another edge, indicating non-projectivity. Emit "**anfangs**" and go up (forced) back to "**sollten**".

- Go down to "**dienen**", down to "**zur**", down to "**lediglich**" and emit it. Go up (forced) to "**zur**", up (unforced) to "**dienen**", emit it, go up (unforced) to "**sollten**", emit it. Go down to "**dienen**", down to "**zur**" emit it, go down to "**Verteidigung**" and emit it.

Correct reordering of this segment would be difficult both for a phrase-based system (since the words are further apart than both the typical maximum distortion distance and maximum phrase length) and for a syntax-based system (due to the presence of non-projectivity and non-tree-locality).

3 Recurrent Neural Network reordering models

Given the reordering framework described above, we could try to directly predict the ex-

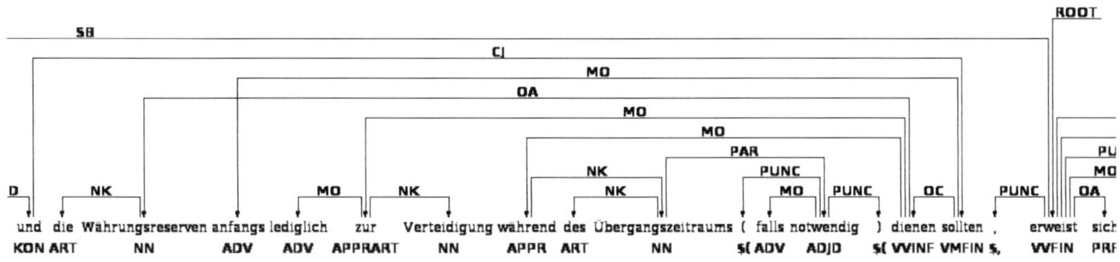

Figure 1: Section of the dependency parse tree of a German sentence.

ecutions as Miceli Barone and Attardi (2013) attempted with their version of the framework. However, the executions of a given sentence can have widely different lengths, which could make incremental inexact decoding such as beam search difficult due to the need to prune over partial hypotheses that have different numbers of emitted words.

Therefore, we decided to investigate a different class of models which have the property that state transition happen only in correspondence with word emission. This enables us to leverage the technology of incremental *language models*.

Using language models for reordering is not something new (Feng et al., 2010), (Durrani et al., 2011), (Bisazza and Federico, 2013), but instead of using a more or less standard n-gram language model, we are going to base our model on *recurrent neural network language models* (Mikolov et al., 2010).

Neural networks allow easy incorporation of multiple types of features and can be trained more specifically on the types of sequences that will occur during decoding, hence they can avoid wasting model space to represent the probabilities of non-permutations.

3.1 Base RNN-RM

Let $f \equiv (f_1, f_2, \ldots, f_{L_f})$ be a source sentence. We model the reordering system as a deterministic single hidden layer recurrent neural network:

$$v(t) = \tau(\Theta^{(1)} \cdot x(t) + \Theta^{REC} \cdot v(t-1)) \quad (4)$$

where $x(t) \in \mathcal{R}^n$ is a feature vector associated to the t-th word in a permutation f', $v(0) \equiv v_{init}$, $\Theta^{(1)}$ and Θ^{REC} are parameters[1] and $\tau(\cdot)$ is the hyperbolic tangent function.

If we know the first $t-1$ words of the permutation f' in order to compute the probability distribution of the t-th word we do the following:

- Iteratively compute the state $v(t-1)$ from the feature vectors $x(1), \ldots, x(t-1)$.
- For the all the indices of the words that haven't occurred in the permutation so far $j \in J(t) \equiv ([1, L_f] - \bar{i}_{t-1:})$, compute a score $h_{j,t} \equiv h_o(v(t-1), x_o(j))$, where $x_o(\cdot)$ is the feature vector of the candidate target word.
- Normalize the scores using the logistic softmax function: $P(\bar{I}_t = j | f, \bar{i}_{t-1:}, t) = \frac{\exp(h_{j,t})}{\sum_{j' \in J(t)} \exp(h_{j',t})}$.

The scoring function $h_o(v(t-1), x_o(j))$ applies a feed-forward hidden layer to the feature inputs $x_o(j)$, and then takes a weighed inner product between the activation of this layer and the state $v(t-1)$. The result is then linearly combined to an additional feature equal to the logarithm of the remaining words in the permutation $(L_f - t)$,[2] and to a bias feature:

$$\begin{aligned} h_{j,t} \equiv &< \tau(\Theta^{(o)} \cdot x_o(j)), \theta^{(2)} \odot v(t-1) > \\ &+ \theta^{(\alpha)} \cdot \log(L_f - t) + \theta^{(bias)} \end{aligned} \quad (5)$$

where $h_{j,t} \equiv h_o(v(t-1), x_o(j))$.

[1] we don't use a bias feature since it is redundant when the layer has input features encoded with the "one-hot" encoding

[2] since we are then passing this score to a softmax of variable size $(L_f - t)$, this feature helps the model to keep the score already approximately scaled.

We can compute the probability of an entire permutation f' just by multiplying the probabilities for each word: $P(f'|f) = P(\bar{I} = \bar{i}|f) = \prod_{t=1}^{L_f} P(\bar{I}_t = \bar{i}_t|f,t)$

3.1.1 Training

Given a training set of pairs of sentences and reference permutations, the training problem is defined as finding the set of parameters $\theta \equiv (v_{init}, \Theta^{(1)}, \theta^{(2)}, \Theta^{REC}, \Theta^{(o)}, \theta^{(\alpha)}, \theta^{(bias)})$ which minimize the per-word empirical cross-entropy of the model w.r.t. the reference permutations in the training set. Gradients can be efficiently computed using *backpropagation through time* (BPTT).

In practice we used the following training architecture:
Stochastic gradient descent, with each training pair (f, f') considered as a single minibatch for updating purposes. Gradients computed using the automatic differentiation facilities of Theano (Bergstra et al., 2010) (which implements a generalized BPTT). No truncation is used. L2-regularization [3]. Learning rates dynamically adjusted per scalar parameter using the *AdaDelta* heuristic (Zeiler, 2012). Gradient clipping heuristic to prevent the "exploding gradient" problem (Graves, 2013). Early stopping w.r.t. a validation set to prevent overfitting. Uniform random initialization for parameters other than the recurrent parameter matrix Θ^{REC}. Random initialization with *echo state property* for Θ^{REC}, with contraction coefficient $\sigma = 0.99$ (Jaeger, 2001), (Gallicchio and Micheli, 2011).

Training time complexity is $O(L_f^2)$ per sentence, which could be reduced to $O(L_f)$ using truncated BTTP at the expense of update accuracy and hence convergence speed. Space complexity is $O(L_f)$ per sentence.

3.1.2 Decoding

In order to use the RNN-RM model for pre-reordering we need to compute the most likely permutation $\overset{*}{f'}$ of the source sentence f:

$$\overset{*}{f'} \equiv \underset{f' \in GEN(f)}{\operatorname{argmax}} P(f'|f) \tag{6}$$

Solving this problem to the global optimum is computationally hard[4], hence we solve it to a local optimum using a *beam search* strategy.

We generate the permutation incrementally from left to right. Starting from an initial state consisting of an empty string and the initial state vector v_{init}, at each step we generate all possible successor states and retain the B-most probable of them (histogram pruning), according to the probability of the entire prefix of permutation they represent.

Since RNN state vectors do not decompose in a meaningful way, we don't use any hypothesis recombination.
At step t there are $L_f - t$ possible successor states, and the process always takes exactly L_f steps[5], therefore time complexity is $O(B \cdot L_f^2)$ and space complexity is $O(B)$.

3.1.3 Features

We use two different feature configurations: *unlexicalized* and *lexicalized*.

In the *unlexicalized* configuration, the state transition input feature function $x(j)$ is composed by the following features, all encoded using the "one-hot" encoding scheme:

- Unigram: $POS(j)$, $DEPREL(j)$, $POS(j) * DEPREL(j)$. Left, right and parent unigram: $POS(k)$, $DEPREL(k)$, $POS(k) * DEPREL(k)$, where k is the index of respectively the word at the left (in the original sentence), at the right and the dependency parent of word j. Unique tags are used for padding.

- Pair features: $POS(j) * POS(k)$, $POS(j) * DEPREL(k)$, $DEPREL(j) * POS(k)$, $DEPREL(j) * DEPREL(k)$, for k defined as above.

[3] $\lambda = 10^{-4}$ on the recurrent matrix, $\lambda = 10^{-6}$ on the final layer, per minibatch.

[4] NP-hard for at least certain choices of features and parameters

[5] actually, $L_f - 1$, since the last choice is forced

- Triple features $POS(j) * POS(left_j) * POS(right_j)$, $POS(j) * POS(left_j) * POS(parent_j)$, $POS(j) * POS(right_j) * POS(parent_j)$.

- Bigram: $POS(j) * POS(k)$, $POS(j) * DEPREL(k)$, $DEPREL(j) * POS(k)$ where k is the previous emitted word in the permutation.

- Topological features: three binary features which indicate whether word j and the previously emitted word are in a parent-child, child-parent or sibling-sibling relation, respectively.

The target word feature function $x_o(j)$ is the same as $x(j)$ except that each feature is also conjoined with a quantized signed distance[6] between word j and the previous emitted word. Feature value combinations that appear less than 100 times in the training set are replaced by a distinguished "rare" tag.

The *lexicalized* configuration is equivalent to the unlexicalized one except that $x(j)$ and $x_o(j)$ also have the surface form of word j (not conjoined with the signed distance).

3.2 Fragment RNN-RM

The *Base RNN-RM* described in the previous section includes dependency information, but not the full information of reordering fragments as defined by our automaton model (sec. 2). In order to determine whether this rich information is relevant to machine translation pre-reordering, we propose an extension, denoted as *Fragment RNN-RM*, which includes reordering fragment features, at expense of a significant increase of time complexity.

We consider a hierarchical recurrent neural network. At top level, this is defined as the previous RNN. However, the $x(j)$ and $x_o(j)$ vectors, in addition to the feature vectors described as above now contain also the final states of another recurrent neural network.

This internal RNN has a separate clock and a separate state vector. For each step t of the top-level RNN which transitions between word $f'(t-1)$ and $f'(t)$, the internal RNN is reinitialized to its own initial state and performs multiple internal steps, one for each action in the fragment of the execution that the walker automaton must perform to walk between words $f'(t-1)$ and $f'(t)$ in the dependency parse (with a special shortcut of length one if they are adjacent in f with monotonic relative order).

The state transition of the inner RNN is defined as:

$$v_r(t) = \tau(\Theta^{(r_1)} \cdot x_r(t_r) + \Theta^{r_{REC}} \cdot v_r(t_r - 1)) \quad (7)$$

where $x_r(t_r)$ is the feature function for the word traversed at inner time t_r in the execution fragment. $v_r(0) = v_r^{init}$, $\Theta^{(r_1)}$ and $\Theta^{r_{REC}}$ are parameters.

Evaluation and decoding are performed essentially in the same was as in Base RNN-RM, except that the time complexity is now $O(L_f^3)$ since the length of execution fragments is $O(L_f)$.

Training is also essentially performed in the same way, though gradient computation is much more involved since gradients propagate from the top-level RNN to the inner RNN. In our implementation we just used the automatic differentiation facilities of Theano.

3.2.1 Features

The *unlexicalized* features for the inner RNN input vector $x_r(t_r)$ depend on the current word in the execution fragment (at index t_r), the previous one and the action label: UP, $DOWN$ or $RIGHT$ (shortcut). $EMIT$ actions are not included as they always implicitly occur at the end of each fragment.

Specifically the features, encoded with the "one-hot" encoding are: $A * POS(t_r) * POS(t_r - 1)$, $A * POS(t_r) * DEPREL(t_r - 1)$, $A * DEPREL(t_r) * POS(t_r - 1)$, $A * DEPREL(t_r) * DEPREL(t_r - 1)$.

These features are also conjoined with the quantized signed distance (in the original sentence) between each pair of words.

The *lexicalized* features just include the surface form of each visited word at t_r.

[6] values greater than 5 and smaller than 10 are quantized as 5, values greater or equal to 10 are quantized as 10. Negative values are treated similarly.

3.3 Base GRU-RM

We also propose a variant of the Base RNN-RM where the standard recurrent hidden layer is replaced by a *Gated Recurrent Unit* layer, recently proposed by Cho et al. (2014) for machine translation applications.
The Base GRU-RM is defined as the Base RNN-RM of sec. 3.1, except that the recurrence relation 4 is replaced by fig. 2

Features are the same of unlexicalized Base RNN-RM (we experienced difficulties training the Base GRU-RM with lexicalized features).
Training is also performed in the same way except that we found more beneficial to convergence speed to optimize using *Adam* (Kingma and Ba, 2014) [7] rather than AdaDelta.
In principle we could also extend the Fragment RNN-RM into a Fragment GRU-RM, but we did not investigate that model in this work.

4 Experiments

We performed German-to-English pre-reordering experiments with Base RNN-RM (both unlexicalized and lexicalized), Fragment RNN-RM and Base GRU-RM .

4.1 Setup

The baseline phrase-based system was trained on the German-to-English corpus included in Europarl v7 (Koehn, 2005). We randomly split it in a 1,881,531 sentence pairs training set, a 2,000 sentence pairs development set (used for tuning) and a 2,000 sentence pairs test set. The English language model was trained on the English side of the parallel corpus augmented with a corpus of sentences from AP News, for a total of 22,891,001 sentences.
The baseline system is phrase-based Moses in a default configuration with maximum distortion distance equal to 6 and lexicalized reordering enabled. Maximum phrase size is equal to 7.
The language model is a 5-gram IRSTLM/KenLM.
The pseudo-oracle system was trained on the training and tuning corpus obtained by permuting the German source side using the heuristic described in section 2.2 and is otherwise equal to the baseline system.
In addition to the test set extracted from Europarl, we also used a 2,525 sentence pairs test set ("news2009") a 3,000 sentence pairs "challenge" set used for the WMT 2013 translation task ("news2013").

We also trained a Moses system with pre-reordering performed by Collins et al. (2005) rules, implemented by Howlett and Dras (2011).
Constituency parsing for Collins et al. (2005) rules was performed with the Berkeley parser (Petrov et al., 2006), while non-projective dependency parsing for our models was performed with the DeSR transition-based parser (Attardi, 2006).

For our experiments, we extract approximately 300,000 sentence pairs from the Moses training set based on a heuristic confidence measure of word-alignment quality (Huang, 2009), (Navratil et al., 2012). We randomly removed 2,000 sentences from this filtered dataset to form a validation set for early stopping, the rest were used for training the pre-reordering models.

4.2 Results

The hidden state size s of the RNNs was set to 100 while it was set to 30 for the GRU model, validation was performed every 2,000 training examples. After 50 consecutive validation rounds without improvement, training was stopped and the set of training parameters that resulted in the lowest validation cross-entropy were saved.
Training took approximately 1.5 days for the unlexicalized Base RNN-RM, 2.5 days for the lexicalized Base RNN-RM and for the unlexicalized Base GRU-RM and 5 days for the unlexicalized Fragment RNN-RM on a 24-core machine without GPU (CPU load never rose to more than 400%).

Decoding was performed with a beam size of 4. Decoding the whole corpus took about 1.0-1.2 days for all the models except Fragment

[7] with learning rate $2 \cdot 10^{-5}$ and all the other hyperparameters equal to the default values in the article.

$$
\begin{aligned}
v_{rst}(t) &= \pi(\Theta_{rst}^{(1)} \cdot x(t) + \Theta_{rst}^{REC} \cdot v(t-1)) \\
v_{upd}(t) &= \pi(\Theta_{upd}^{(1)} \cdot x(t) + \Theta_{upd}^{REC} \cdot v(t-1)) \\
v_{raw}(t) &= \tau(\Theta^{(1)} \cdot x(t) + \Theta^{REC} \cdot v(t-1) \odot v_{upd}(t)) \\
v(t) &= v_{rst}(t) \odot v(t-1) + (1 - v_{rst}(t)) \odot v_{raw}(t)
\end{aligned}
\tag{8}
$$

Figure 2: GRU recurrence equations. $v_{rst}(t)$ and $v_{upd}(t)$ are the activation vectors of the "reset" and "update" gates, respectively, and $\pi(\cdot)$ is the logistic sigmoid function.

Reordering	BLEU	improvement
none	62.10	
unlex. Base RNN-RM	64.03	+1.93
lex. Base RNN-RM	63.99	+1.89
unlex. Fragment RNN-RM	64.43	+2.33
unlex. Base GRU-RM	64.78	+2.68

Figure 3: "Monolingual" reordering scores (upstream system output vs. "oracle"-permuted German) on the Europarl test set. All improvements are significant at 1% level.

RNN-RM for which it took about 3 days.

Effects on monolingual reordering score are shown in fig. 3, effects on translation quality are shown in fig. 4.

4.3 Discussion and analysis

All our models significantly improve over the phrase-based baseline, performing as well as or almost as well as (Collins et al., 2005), which is an interesting result since our models doesn't require any specific linguistic expertise.

Surprisingly, the lexicalized version of Base RNN-RM performed worse than the unlexicalized one. This goes contrary to expectation as neural language models are usually lexicalized and in fact often use nothing but lexical features.

The unlexicalized Fragment RNN-RM was quite accurate but very expensive both during training and decoding, thus it may not be practical.

The unlexicalized Base GRU-RM performed very well, especially on the Europarl dataset (where all the scores are much higher than the other datasets) and it never performed significantly worse than the unlexicalized Fragment RNN-RM which is much slower.

We also performed exploratory experiments with different feature sets (such as lexical-only features) but we couldn't obtain a good training error. Larger network sizes should increase model capacity and may possibly enable training on simpler feature sets.

5 Conclusions

We presented a class of statistical syntax-based pre-reordering systems for machine translation.

Our systems processes source sentences parsed with non-projective dependency parsers and permutes them into a target-like word order, suitable for translation by an appropriately trained downstream phrase-based system.

The models we proposed are completely trained with machine learning approaches and is, in principle, capable of generating arbitrary permutations, without the hard constraints that are commonly present in other statistical syntax-based pre-reordering methods.

Practical constraints depend on the choice of features and are therefore quite flexible, allowing a trade-off between accuracy and speed.

In our experiments with the RNN-RM and

Test set	system	BLEU	improvement
Europarl	baseline	33.00	
Europarl	"oracle"	41.80	+8.80
Europarl	Collins	33.52	+0.52
Europarl	unlex. Base RNN-RM	33.41	+0.41
Europarl	lex. Base RNN-RM	33.38	+0.38
Europarl	unlex. Fragment RNN-RM	33.54	+0.54
Europarl	**unlex. Base GRU-RM**	34.15	**+1.15**
news2013	baseline	18.80	
news2013	Collins	NA	NA
news2013	unlex. Base RNN-RM	19.19	+0.39
news2013	lex. Base RNN-RM	19.01	+0.21
news2013	unlex. Fragment RNN-RM	19.27	+0.47
news2013	**unlex. Base GRU-RM**	19.28	**+0.48**
news2009	baseline	18.09	
news2009	**Collins**	18.74	**+0.65**
news2009	unlex. Base RNN-RM	18.50	+0.41
news2009	lex. Base RNN-RM	18.44	+0.35
news2009	unlex. Fragment RNN-RM	18.60	+0.51
news2009	unlex. Base GRU-RM	18.58	+0.49

Figure 4: RNN-RM translation scores. All improvements are significant at 1% level.

GRU-RM models we managed to achieve translation quality improvements comparable to those of the best hand-coded pre-reordering rules.

References

Yaser Al-Onaizan and Kishore Papineni. 2006. Distortion models for statistical machine translation. In *Proceedings of the 21st International Conference on Computational Linguistics and the 44th Annual Meeting of the Association for Computational Linguistics*, ACL-44, pages 529–536, Stroudsburg, PA, USA. Association for Computational Linguistics.

Giuseppe Attardi. 2006. Experiments with a multilanguage non-projective dependency parser. In *Proceedings of the Tenth Conference on Computational Natural Language Learning*, CoNLL-X '06, pages 166–170, Stroudsburg, PA, USA. Association for Computational Linguistics.

James Bergstra, Olivier Breuleux, Frédéric Bastien, Pascal Lamblin, Razvan Pascanu, Guillaume Desjardins, Joseph Turian, David Warde-Farley, and Yoshua Bengio. 2010. Theano: a CPU and GPU math expression compiler. In *Proceedings of the Python for Scientific Computing Conference (SciPy)*, June. Oral Presentation.

Alexandra Birch, Miles Osborne, and Philipp Koehn. 2008. Predicting success in machine translation. In *Proceedings of the Conference on Empirical Methods in Natural Language Processing*, EMNLP '08, pages 745–754, Stroudsburg, PA, USA. Association for Computational Linguistics.

Arianna Bisazza and Marcello Federico. 2013. Efficient solutions for word reordering in German-English phrase-based statistical machine translation. In *Proceedings of the Eighth Workshop on Statistical Machine Translation*, pages 440–451, Sofia, Bulgaria, August. Association for Computational Linguistics.

Cristina Bosco and Vincenzo Lombardo. 2004. Dependency and relational structure in treebank annotation. In *COLING 2004 Recent Advances in Dependency Grammar*, pages 1–8.

Kyunghyun Cho, Bart van Merriënboer, Dzmitry Bahdanau, and Yoshua Bengio. 2014. On the properties of neural machine translation: Encoder-decoder approaches. *arXiv preprint arXiv:1409.1259*.

Michael Collins, Philipp Koehn, and Ivona Kučerová. 2005. Clause restructuring for statistical machine translation. In *Proceedings of the 43rd annual meeting on association for computational linguistics*, pages 531–540. Association for Computational Linguistics.

Nadir Durrani, Helmut Schmid, and Alexander Fraser. 2011. A joint sequence translation model with integrated reordering. In *Proceedings of the 49th Annual Meeting of the Association for Computational Linguistics: Human Language Technologies-Volume 1*, pages 1045–1054. Association for Computational Linguistics.

Chris Dyer and Philip Resnik. 2010. Context-free reordering, finite-state translation. In *Human Language Technologies: The 2010 Annual Conference of the North American Chapter of the Association for Computational Linguistics*, HLT '10, pages 858–866, Stroudsburg, PA, USA. Association for Computational Linguistics.

Minwei Feng, Arne Mauser, and Hermann Ney. 2010. A source-side decoding sequence model for statistical machine translation. In *Conference of the Association for Machine Translation in the Americas (AMTA)*.

C. Gallicchio and A. Micheli. 2011. Architectural and markovian factors of echo state networks. *Neural Networks*, 24(5):440 – 456.

Dmitriy Genzel. 2010. Automatically learning source-side reordering rules for large scale machine translation. In *Proceedings of the 23rd International Conference on Computational Linguistics*, COLING '10, pages 376–384, Stroudsburg, PA, USA. Association for Computational Linguistics.

Alex Graves. 2013. Generating sequences with recurrent neural networks. *arXiv preprint arXiv:1308.0850*.

Susan Howlett and Mark Dras. 2011. Clause restructuring for SMT not absolutely helpful. In *Proceedings of the 49th Annual Meeting of the Assocation for Computational Linguistics: Human Language Technologies*, pages 384–388.

Fei Huang. 2009. Confidence measure for word alignment. In *Proceedings of the Joint Conference of the 47th Annual Meeting of the ACL and the 4th International Joint Conference on Natural Language Processing of the AFNLP: Volume 2-Volume 2*, pages 932–940. Association for Computational Linguistics.

Herbert Jaeger. 2001. The echo state approach to analysing and training recurrent neural networks-with an erratum note. *Bonn, Germany: German National Research Center for Information Technology GMD Technical Report*, 148:34.

Maxim Khalilov and José AR Fonollosa. 2011. Syntax-based reordering for statistical machine translation. *Computer speech & language*, 25(4):761–788.

Diederik Kingma and Jimmy Ba. 2014. Adam: A method for stochastic optimization. *arXiv preprint arXiv:1412.6980*.

Philipp Koehn, Hieu Hoang, Alexandra Birch, Chris Callison-Burch, Marcello Federico, Nicola Bertoldi, Brooke Cowan, Wade Shen, Christine Moran, Richard Zens, Chris Dyer, Ondřej Bojar, Alexandra Constantin, and Evan Herbst. 2007. Moses: open source toolkit for statistical machine translation. In *Proceedings of the 45th Annual Meeting of the ACL on Interactive Poster and Demonstration Sessions*, ACL '07, pages 177–180, Stroudsburg, PA, USA. Association for Computational Linguistics.

Philipp Koehn. 2005. Europarl: A parallel corpus for statistical machine translation. In *Conference Proceedings: the tenth Machine Translation Summit*, pages 79–86, Phuket, Thailand. AAMT, AAMT.

Uri Lerner and Slav Petrov. 2013. Source-side classifier preordering for machine translation. In *Proceedings of the 2014 Conference on Empirical Methods in Natural Language Processing (EMNLP '13)*.

Antonio Valerio Miceli Barone and Giuseppe Attardi. 2013. Pre-reordering for machine translation using transition-based walks on dependency parse trees. In *Proceedings of the Eighth Workshop on Statistical Machine Translation*, pages 164–169, Sofia, Bulgaria, August. Association for Computational Linguistics.

Tomas Mikolov, Martin Karafiát, Lukas Burget, Jan Cernockỳ, and Sanjeev Khudanpur. 2010. Recurrent neural network based language model. In *INTERSPEECH*, pages 1045–1048.

Jiri Navratil, Karthik Visweswariah, and Ananthakrishnan Ramanathan. 2012. A comparison of syntactic reordering methods for english-german machine translation. In *COLING*, pages 2043–2058.

Franz Josef Och, Christoph Tillmann, Hermann Ney, et al. 1999. Improved alignment models for statistical machine translation. In *Proc. of the Joint SIGDAT Conf. on Empirical Methods in Natural Language Processing and Very Large Corpora*, pages 20–28.

Slav Petrov, Leon Barrett, Romain Thibaux, and Dan Klein. 2006. Learning accurate, compact, and interpretable tree annotation. In *Proceedings of the 21st International Conference on Computational Linguistics and the 44th annual meeting of the Association for Computational Linguistics*, pages 433–440. Association for Computational Linguistics.

Roy Tromble and Jason Eisner. 2009. Learning linear ordering problems for better translation. In *Proceedings of the 2009 Conference on Empirical Methods in Natural Language Processing: Volume 2 - Volume 2*, EMNLP '09, pages 1007–1016, Stroudsburg, PA, USA. Association for Computational Linguistics.

Karthik Visweswariah, Rajakrishnan Rajkumar, Ankur Gandhe, Ananthakrishnan Ramanathan, and Jiri Navratil. 2011. A word reordering model for improved machine translation. In *Proceedings of the Conference on Empirical Methods in Natural Language Processing*, EMNLP '11, pages 486–496, Stroudsburg, PA, USA. Association for Computational Linguistics.

Matthew D Zeiler. 2012. Adadelta: An adaptive learning rate method. *arXiv preprint arXiv:1212.5701*.

Translating Negation: Induction, Search And Model Errors

Federico Fancellu and Bonnie Webber
School of Informatics
University of Edinburgh
11 Crichton Street, Edinburgh
f.fancellu[at]sms.ed.ac.uk, bonnie[at]inf.ed.ac.uk

Abstract

Statistical Machine Translation systems show considerably worse performance in translating negative sentences than positive ones (Fancellu and Webber, 2014; Wetzel and Bond, 2012). Various techniques have addressed the problem of translating negation, but their underlying assumptions have never been validated by a proper error analysis. A related paper (Fancellu and Webber, 2015) reports on a manual error analysis of the *kinds* of errors involved in translating negation. The present paper presents ongoing work to discover their *causes* by considering which, if any, are *induction*, *search* or *model* errors. We show that standard *oracle decoding* techniques provide little help due to the locality of negation scope and their reliance on a single reference. We are working to address these weaknesses using a chart analysis based on *oracle hypotheses*, guided by the negation elements contained in a source span and by how these elements are expected to be translated at each decoding step. Preliminary results show chart analysis is able to give a more in-depth analysis of the above errors and better explains the results of the manual analysis.

1 Introduction

In recent years there has been increasing interest in improving the quality of SMT systems over a wide range of linguistic phenomena, including coreference resolution (Hardmeier et al., 2014) and modality (Baker et al., 2012). Negation, however, is a problem that has still not been researched thoroughly (section 2).

Our previous study (Fancellu and Webber, 2015) takes a first step towards understanding why negation is a problem in SMT, through manual analysis of the kinds of errors involved in its translation. Our error analysis employs a small set of standard string-based operations, applying them to the semantic elements involved in the meaning of negation (section 3).

The current paper describes our current work on understanding the causes of these errors. Focussing on the distinction between *induction*, *search* and *model errors*, we point out the challenges in trying to use existing techniques to quantify these three types of errors in the context of translating negation.

Previous work on ascribing errors to induction, search, or model has taken an approach using oracle decoding, i.e. forcing the decoder to reconstruct the reference sentence as a proxy to analyse its potentiality. We show however that this technique does not suit well semantic phenomena with *local* scope (such as negation), given that a conclusion drawn on the reconstruction of an entire sentence might refer to spans not related to these. Moreover, as in previous work, we stress once again the limitation of using a single reference to compute the oracle (section 4.1)

To overcome these problems, we propose the use of an *oracle hypothesis*, instead of an *oracle sentence*, that relies uniquely on the negation elements contained in the source span and *how these are expected to be translated in the target hypothesis* at a given time during decoding (section 4.2).

Sections 5 and 6 report results of the analysis on a Chinese-to-English Hierarchical Phrase Based

Proceedings of SSST-9, Ninth Workshop on Syntax, Semantics and Structure in Statistical Translation, pages 21–29,
Denver, Colorado, June 4, 2015.

Model (Chiang, 2007). We show that even if it possible to detect the presence of model errors through the use of an oracle sentence, computing an oracle hypotheses at each step during decoding offers a more robust, in-depth analysis around the problem of translating negation and helps explaining the errors observed during the manual analysis.

2 Previous Work

While recent years have seen work on automatically detecting negation in monolingual texts (Chowdhury and Mahbub, 2012; Read et al., 2012), SMT has mainly considered it a side problem. For this reason, no actual analysis on the type of errors involved in translating negation or their causes has been specifically carried out. The standard approach has been to formulate a hypothesis about what can go wrong when translating negation, modify the SMT system in a way aimed at reducing the number of times that happens, and then assume that any increase in BLEU score - the standard automatic evaluation metric used in SMT - confirms the initial hypothesis. Collins et al. (2005) and Li et al. (2009) considers negation, along with other linguistic phenomena, as a problem of *structural mismatch* between source and target; Wetzel and Bond (2012) considers it instead as a problem of *training data sparsity*; finally Baker et al. (2012) and Fancellu and Webber (2014) considers it as a *model problem*, where the system needs enhancement with respect to the semantics of negation.

Only a few efforts have tried to investigate errors occurring during decoding. Automatic evaluation metrics are in fact only informative about the quality of the output, but not about the decoding process that produces the output. As such, the most relevant related work are two studies on the main categories of errors during decoding (Auli et al., 2009; Wisniewski and Yvon, 2013). Both works use the reference sentence as a proxy to generate an oracle hypothesis but they differ in the technique they use and in the problem they are interesting analysing. Auli et al. (2009) targets induction errors — i.e. cases where a good translation is absent from the search space — by forcing the decoder to generate the reference sentence with varying translation options (for each source span) and distortion limits. If when increasing the number of target translations considered for each span, the number of references that is possible to fully generate also increases, an induction error has occurred. Results on a French-to-English PBSMT validates this hypothesis.

Wisniewski and Yvon (2013) considers instead oracle decoding as a proxy to distinguish search vs. model errors. If the oracle translation has a model score higher than the 1-best system output, a search error has occurred, since the system could not output the hypothesis with the highest probability; in contrast, a model error has occurred when the scoring function is unable to rank translations correctly. Here, the oracle translation is generated via ILP by maximising the unigram recall between oracle and reference translation, resembling the work of Germann et al. (2001) on optimal decoding in word-based models. In both Auli et al. (2009) and Wisniewski and Yvon (2013), almost all the errors during decoding are model errors.

A shortcoming of both methods is that neither can generate more than 35% of the references in the test set, by virtue of taking only one particular reference as the oracle, despite there usually being many ways that a source sentence can be translated.

3 Manual Error Analysis

This section briefly summarises the key points of the manual error analysis described in (Fancellu and Webber, 2015), since they also underpin the automated analysis described in section 4. The manual error analysis makes two assumptions:

- the semantic structure of negation can be annotated in a similar way across different languages, because the essentials of negation are language-independent.
- for analytic languages like English and Chinese, a set of string-based operations (*deletion*, *insertion* and *reordering*) can be used to assess translation errors in the semantics of negation.

Both assumptions involve first of all reducing a rather abstract semantic phenomenon into elements tangible at string-level. Following Blanco and Moldoval (2011), Morante and Blanco (2012) and Fancellu and Webber (2014), we decompose negation into its three main components, described below, and use them as the target of our analysis.

- **Cue**, i.e. the word or multi-words unit inherently expressing negation (e.g. 'He is not washing his clothes')

- **Event**, i.e. the lexical event the cue directly refers to (e.g. 'He is not washing his clothes)

- **Scope**, i.e. all the elements whose falsity would prove the statement to be true (e.g. 'He is not washing his clothes'); the event is taken to be part of the scope, since its falsity influences the truth value of negation. In the error analysis however, we exclude the event from the scope (since it is already considered *per se*) and further decompose the scope, to isolate the **semantic fillers** in its boundaries (*He*, *his clothes*), here taken to be Propbank-like semantic roles.

Given that we are combining standard, widely used error categories and language-independent semantic elements, we expect the annotation process and the error analysis to be robust and applicable to languages other than English and Chinese.

Results show an in-depth analysis of negation-related errors, where we are able to discern clearly which operations affect which elements and to what extent. We found the cue the element the least prone to translation errors with only four cases of it being deleted during translation. We also found reordering to be the most frequent error category especially for the fillers, given that the SMT system does not possess explicit knowledge of semantic frames and its boundaries.

By making use of the decoding trace, containing the rules used to build the 1-best hypothesis, we could also inspect the causes of deletion and insertion. We found that almost all deletion and insertion errors are caused by a wrong rule application that translates a Chinese source span containing negation into an English hypothesis that does not or vice versa. OOV items seem *not* to constitute a problem when translating negation. This is important especially in the case of the *cue*, whose absence means that the whole negation instance is lost. Given that all the cues in the test set have been seen during training, we also know the system has the ability to *potentially* reproduce negation on the target side.

4 Automatic Error Analysis

The manual error analysis can only get us as far as analysing the 1-best hypothesis and its building blocks. No explicit information on the causes of these errors can be recovered from the decoding trace only. To address this problem, we introduce two different techniques to analyse and distinguish different kinds of errors occurring at decoding time.

First however, we give a more formal definition of the three main categories of decoding-related errors as follows, where e and $p(e)$ are the optimal translation the decoder can produce, along with its probability while $\hat{e}$ and $p(\hat{e})$ stand for the 1-best output and its probability.

- **Search error**: $e \neq \hat{e}$ and $p(e) > p(\hat{e})$; the 1-best output is not the most probable output, given the model. Search errors are a consequence of the impossibility of exploring the entire search space, where more probable hypothesis may have been pruned.

- **Model error**: $e \neq \hat{e}$ and $p(e) < p(\hat{e})$; the model scores a semantically sub-optimal translation higher than the optimal one. This is because the scoring function lacks relevant features or the features present have not been properly weighted.

- **Induction error**: e cannot be generated because its components (phrases or rules) are absent from the search space.

4.1 Constrained Decoding

The first technique involves forcing the decoder to reproduce reference sentences if they contain negation. It reflects the assumption that if the system is able to reconstruct such oracles, it is *potentially* able to translate negation correctly.

We use the *constrained decoding* feature included in Moses (Koehn et al., 2007) to this purpose. In its basic implementation, constrained decoding assesses the degree of overlap between hypothesis and reference sentence; given a source span, the feature function assigns a score to each of the target hypothesis as follows:

$$s_{constrDec} = \begin{cases} 1 & \text{if } \exists\, h \in H_p \wedge h \in R_p \\ -\infty & \text{if } \nexists\, h \in H_p \wedge h \in R_p \end{cases}$$

where h is a phrase in the hypothesis phrase set H_p and R_p is the set of reference phrases.

Constrained decoding can potentially reveal induction errors and distinguish between search and model errors. Following Auli et al. (2009), we try to increase the *translation option limit* parameter which determines how many target translations are considered for each source span; if larger values lead to the system being able to decode more references, induction errors are occurring. Using the same heuristics as Wisniewski and Yvon (2013), we can also distinguish between search error vs. model errors by checking whether the oracle has a total model score higher than the previous 1-best output or vice versa.

We also take into consideration the interaction between induction and search errors. A bigger search space would be needed in order to consider more target hypotheses per source span during decoding. Thus we experiment by combining different translation option limits and cube pruning pop limits, where the latter limits the number of hypotheses that can be inserted in each cell's stack, which in turn influences the size of the search space.

There is however a potential pitfall when applying these heuristics to the analysis of negation-related errors. Chances are in fact that negation does not scope over the entire reference sentence, as exemplified in (1), where only the first portion of the source and the last portion in the reference contain an instance of negation.

(1) *Src:* *jǐnánjūnqū* *mǒu*
Jinan military region some
bù *bànshì* *gōngkāi* *shǐ*
department business make public make
[*rèdiǎn*]$_{scope}$ *bù*$_{cue}$ *rè*$_{event}$
hot spots not hot
Ref: [Hotspots]$_{scope}$ not$_{cue}$ hot$_{event}$ due to transparent business procedures in Jinan military region

Given that negation can be (and usually is) a semantic phenomenon with a *local* scope, if the decoder fails to reproduce (1), one cannot simply conclude that negation-related elements cannot be reproduced. Moreover, because the oracle translation may involve elements outside the scope of negation, constrained decoding does not permit one to draw any conclusion about the kind of error that has occurred in the case of negation.

In order to overcome this problem, we try to isolate the elements of negation in both source and reference and run constrained decoding on those portions only. However, doing so demands we assume that negation is represented similarly in both source and the reference sentences. This is however not different from the general problem around *oracle decoding*, i.e. considering one reference sentence as the only ground truth. *Constrained decoding* is in fact an alignment problem, where we try to maximise the presence of reference segments in decoding, giving the source spans. If the reference spans are only paraphrases of the source spans, not direct translations, it is unlikely that the system will be able to reconstruct the oracle. Negation is not an exception, given the many ways that the same negation instance can be paraphrased. This is exemplified in (2) where the event is rendered in Chinese as an adjectival predicate (*lǐxiǎng* → 'ideal') while it is translated non-literally in the reference sentence as a nominal predicate ('*what it should be*').

(2) *Src:* [...] [*rénmen de jīngshén* *jiànkāng*
[...] people of psychology health
hěn]$_{scope}$ *bù*$_{cue}$ *lǐxiǎng*$_{event}$ [...]
very not ideal [...]
Ref: [...] [people's psychological health is]$_{scope}$ not$_{cue}$ [at all]$_{scope}$ what it should be$_{event}$ [...]

4.2 Chart Analysis

Constrained decoding demands the obviously false assumption that there is only one correct translation of a given source sentence. It also provides no alternative to assuming that conclusions formulated from those few references the system is able to reconstruct, also apply to the rest of the negated instances. Finally and most importantly, it is hard to explain the results obtained from the manual error analysis by simply reconstructing an oracle sentence and if it is really a case of model errors, there is no way to know which model component (i.e. score) is the most responsible for a bad ranking of the hypothesis translations.

The approach we sketch out in this section tries to abstract from having a single reference and relies instead of *what is expected* to be translated at a given time during decoding. The end goal here is to compute *oracle hypotheses*, instead of *oracle sentences*.

We start by formulating four main expectations when translating instances of negation:

1. The **cue** has to be present
2. The **event** has to be correctly translated
3. The **cue** has to be attached to the correct **event**
4. The **fillers** have to be included in the right scope and connected to the right event in such way that they take the same (or an equivalent) semantic role to the one they had in the source.

Expectations (1) and (2) are related to the presence of a given element and allows us to analyse those instances of *deletions* observed in the manual error analysis; in (3) and (4), we investigate instead whether negation elements are grouped under the correct scope, therefore focusing on *reordering* errors.

If we know *at what time* during decoding we are translating a negation element, we can make use of these expectations; if a source sentence of length l contains a negation element in a span $S = s_n...s_m$ where $0 \leq n \leq m < l$ and given that cells in the decoding chart are indexed by the span they cover in the source, we expect that in cell $[i\text{-}j]$, where $i \leq n \leq m \leq j$, the target hypotheses must contain a projection of this element and the two must be aligned.

Given these two assumptions, a comparison with constrained decoding is quite straight-forward. Meeting these expectations is the same as computing an oracle, but instead of doing it at sentence level, we do that at a hypothesis level (hence the name *oracle hypothesis*), that is, for each covered span in the source (here taken to be a cell in the chart).

The scores for each hypothesis in the cell provide detailed information about the presence of model errors; since we expect hypotheses that satisfy the four expectations above to be scored (and ranked) higher than those which do not, we can not only calculate the number of times this is not the case, but we can only see how low in the rankings a good translation is and which features cause this failure. By varying the *translation options limit* and the *cube pruning pop limit* parameter, we can also investigate whether these expectations are not met because of search and induction errors. Even if the search space is so vast that it is practically impossible to explore it all, we assume that with a large upper bound of hypotheses per stack, we are able to capture all relevant errors, and if any are not captured, they can be attributed to the "long tail" of rare occurrences.

The main two challenges at this point are to know (a) which elements in the source are negation elements and (b) whether they are translated correctly in the target hypothesis. In the case of (a) we use the manual annotation presented in (Fancellu and Webber, 2015). Future work will try to automate the process.

Challenge (b) requires a way to compute those expectations on the target (English) side. In order to detect the presence of a cue, we build a list of English negation cues from the training data using the exact same heuristics and training data as Chowdhury and Mahbub (2012) and check whether a given hypothesis contains a cue from this list. In order to deal with those cases of *lexical negation* where cues in the source are rendered as part of the meaning of a word in the target (e.g. zh: ***bù****tóng* → en: '*different*'), we extract a mapping between Chinese cues and these words covertly expressing negation from the manually aligned GALE Chinese-English Word Alignment and Tagging Training data (Li et al., 2012).

In order to recognise the presence of a correct event, it is possible to check whether the hypothesis contains a good translation of the source using bilingual dictionaries (e.g. CCEDIT[1]) and enriching the results through synonyms (e.g. WordNet) and paraphrases databases (e.g. PPDB (Ganitkevitch et al., 2013)).

To ensure that the cue refers to the right event, we use the Stanford dependency parse (Manning, 2008) and apply it to each of the target (English) hypothesis in the cell's stack to check whether a subordinate-head relation is established between the two. Given

[1]http://www.mdbg.net/chindict/chindict.php?page=cedict

that the Stanford parser does not build a *neg* relationship from each negation cue to its head event, we just check more in general whether the cue is in a subordinate relationship with the event.

Finally, we use the dependency parse to verify that the fillers are correctly connected to negated event. This is a problem that needs more consideration and is therefore left for future work. The correct rendering of the fillers in the negation scope is in fact related to the more general open-problem of preserving predicate-argument structure during translation.

We are also exploring a second approach where we detect these elements on the English side by generating as many paraphrases as possible from the reference sentences using the same approach of (Zhao et al., 2009) and the PPDB database. We then extract cues, events and fillers from these paraphrases automatically and check whether they are present in the chart hypotheses and they correctly relate to each other.

5 System

We carried out the error analysis on the output of the Chinese-to-English hierarchical phrase based system submitted by the University of Edinburgh for the NIST12 MT evaluation campaign. The system was trained on ~2.1 millions length-filtered segments in the news domain, with 44678806 tokens on the source and 50452704 on the target, with MGIZA++ (Gao and Vogel, 2008) used for alignment. The Chinese side of the training and the test set were segmented using the LDCWordSegmenter. The system was tuned using MERT (Och, 2003) on the NIST06 set.

The automatic error analysis was carried out on a sub-set of 54 segments the NIST MT08 test set[2], each containing at least an instance of negation on the source side. Although small, this set was considered to be representative given that it clearly shows a pattern in the errors involved in translation negation.

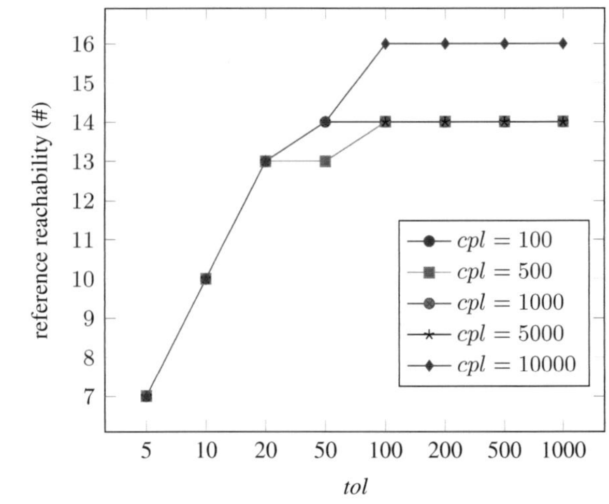

Figure 1: Number of reachable oracle negation instances plotted against the *translation option limit* (*tol*) for each of the five *cube pruning pop limit* (*cpl*).

6 Results

In this section we present the results related to the two methods introduced in sect. 4.

As shown in Figure 1, given the default settings of our decoder (*tol*: 20; *cpl*: 1000), we were able to generate only 13 out of 54 references in the test set (24%). Increasing the *translation options limit* to 100 leads only to a slight improvement and an upper bound of 16 reachable references (29%). We also did not see any noteworthy interaction between *translation option limit* and *cube pruning pop limit* (where *cpl* values of 500 and 1000 track the graph for a *cpl* of 5000); if there is no need for a large number of hypotheses to be considered during decoding to reconstruct the reference, there is also no need for a bigger search space.

Finally, comparison of the total model score of the oracle hypothesis vs. the 1-best output shows that in all cases the score of latter is higher than the former. We can conclude that for the references the system was able to reconstruct, model errors are a major cause of failure whilst induction and search errors are not. However, the number of references the system was able to fully reconstruct is very low, which makes it hard to draw final conclusions from constrained decoding alone, including any connection between these results and our manual error analysis. We present here preliminary results for the chart

[2]This sub-set containing only negative sentences was extracted during the manual evaluation. Out of 1357 segments in the NIST MT08 set, we randomly picked 250 segments and annotate all instances of negation whether present

analysis approach. We focus on detecting an *oracle hypothesis* that contain a right translation of the *cue* (therefore satisfying only expectation 1 in sect. 5.2).

Our first goal is to identify those cases where the cue is absent in the final cell, since deletion was the only type of error that involved the cue. However, in general, we want to have a measure of how strong our model is when translating the negation cue. A good model should in fact always be able to correctly translate a cue whether present in the source span.

We found that there are a total of 14948 cells for the whole test set where a translation of the cue is expected (i.e. the source contains a cue in the span the cell covers), for an average of ~277 cells per sentence. We found that in 8311 of those cells (~57%), a projection of the cue is absent, four of which are final, meaning that the cue is absent from four of the hypothesis translations output by the system. However, a per sentence distribution of the cells where the cue is expected but absent (Figure 2) shows that there is at least one cell in a chart containing the correct cue. Conversely, in no chart is the cue is completely absent. This means that in all cases the cue was reproduced at same point but in some, it failed to propagate to the final cell. This shows that chart analysis is useful to explain those cases of cue-related errors found in the manual analysis. We can conclude that the system is always *potentially* able to translate the cue. Given that there is no shortage of rules to translate the cue with default parameters, we can also conclude that, for the negation element here considered, no induction error has occurred. This conclusion is more solid than the one drawn from the constrained decoding approach, since it is based on the analysis of the decoding process for the entire test set.

We also found that in each cell an hypothesis containing the right translation of the *cue* is, on average, ranked highly (2.79, where 0 represents the 1-best hypothesis). Out of the 1100 cases where the 1-best hypothesis and the cue-translation *oracle hypothesis* are not the same, the times the scores of the former are higher than the latter are: 275 for LM score (25%), 730 for the indirect translation probability (**66%**), 718 for the indirect lexical probability (**65.2%**), 525 for the direct translation probability (47.7%) and 435 for the direct lexical probability

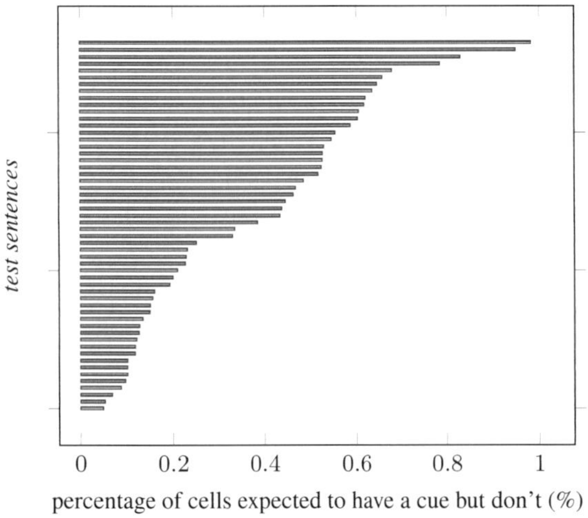

Figure 2: Distribution of cells per sentence *not* containing the expected *cue*.

(39.5%). Chart analysis can show us which features are the most responsible for *model errors*. We found out that the translation model holds the main responsibility for incorrectly ranking hypotheses containing the correct cue projection. Again, this useful form of analysis could not have been carried out using *constrained decoding* alone.

Finally, we are left to consider the impact of *search errors* in translating the negation cue. We first check whether these are involved in the four cases in which the cue is absent from the system's output translation, by testing with larger *cube pruning pop limit* and *translation options limit* values. Results shows that even by considering large values (of 10000 and 1000 respectively), no cue translations was found in the final cell of the chart for those sentences where deletion occurs. Enlarging the *search space* does not lead to any more cue translations making it to the final cell of the chart, highlighting the fact that translation of cue does not involve *search errors*.

7 Conclusion

In the present paper, we presented ongoing work on analysing the *causes* of the errors involved in translating negation, targeting three main categories: **induction**, **search** and **model** errors.

Following previous work, we applied an *oracle decoding*-based technique to detect those errors by forcing the decoder the generate the reference sentence. Conclusions drawn from the references the decoder could reconstruct show that translating negation primarily involve model errors. However, the technique has two important limitations: (a) drawing conclusion from the reachability of an entire reference sentence is not informative when analysing semantic phenomena that usually have a *local* scope, such as negation; (b) the oracle is taken to be one reference sentence, while there are usually many ways to translate a sentence correctly and therefore (c) the results obtained applies to only part of the test set and cannot be taken to represent the entire data; (d) being able to generate an oracle does not give any in-depth insight on the each decoding step which is detrimental if we have to explain the results from the manual analysis.

Given these shortcomings, we sketch out an analysis that is able to compute partial *oracle hypotheses*, given the negation elements contained in a source span and four main *expectations* related to how negation elements should be translated at a given time during decoding. Preliminary results on *cue* translation show that the system can *potentially* translate all the cues in all the test sentences. No induction or search errors were found meaning that *model errors* are the only category of errors occurred in translating the negation cue. Moreover, a comparison between 1-best and *oracle* hypotheses show that the translation model scores are the main responsible for bad ranking. In general, it was shown that our method is able to give a more in-depth analysis of the process of translating negation at decoding time.

8 Future Work

In the present work, we have only presented the general idea around considering *oracle hypotheses* instead of *oracle sentences*, along with some preliminary results. Further work is however necessary to complete the analysis of the other two elements of negation – **event** and **fillers**.

It is worth remembering several factors can impact the kind of errors found in translation. Hierarchical phrase-based models are in fact non-purely syntax driven methods that are able to deal with high levels of reordering. That however also means that (a) there is no concept of constituent boundaries and (b) when reordering is performed incorrectly there is a high degree of element scrambling. We therefore accept that system-related proprieties might influence the presence of one error class over another and it will therefore be useful to conduct the same analysis on different models. In the same way, different languages will also display different problems and it is therefore necessary to consider the choice of language pair as another variable that can influence the result of such analysis.

9 Acknowledgements

This work was supported by the Accept, MosesCore and GRAM+ grants. The authors would like to thank Adam Lopez for his comments and suggestions and the two anonymous reviewers for their feedback.

References

Auli, M., Lopez, A., Hoang, H., and Koehn, P. (2009). A systematic analysis of translation model search spaces. In *Proceedings of the Fourth Workshop on Statistical Machine Translation*, pages 224–232.

Baker, K., Bloodgood, M., Dorr, B. J., Callison-Burch, C., Filardo, N. W., Piatko, C., Levin, L., and Miller, S. (2012). Modality and negation in SIMT use of modality and negation in semantically-informed syntactic MT. *Computational Linguistics*, 38(2):411–438.

Blanco, E. and Moldoval, D. (2011). Some Issues on Detecting Negation from Text. In *Proceedings of the 24th Florida Artificial Intelligence Research Society Conference (FLAIRS-24)*, pages 228–233, Palm Beach, FL, USA.

Chiang, D. (2007). Hierarchical phrase-based translation. *Computational linguistics*, 33(2):201–228.

Chowdhury, M. and Mahbub, F. (2012). FBK: Exploiting phrasal and contextual clues for negation scope detection. In *Proceedings of the First Joint Conference on Lexical and Computational Semantics-Volume 1: Proceedings of the main conference and the shared task, and Volume 2: Proceedings of the Sixth International Workshop on Semantic Evaluation*, pages 340–346.

Collins, M., Koehn, P., and Kučerová, I. (2005). Clause restructuring for statistical machine translation. In *Proceedings of the 43rd annual meeting on association for computational linguistics*, pages 531–540.

Fancellu, F. and Webber, B. (2014). Applying the semantics of negation to SMT through n-best list re-ranking. *EACL 2014*, page 598.

Fancellu, F. and Webber, B. (2015). Translating negation: A manual error analysis. In *Workshop On Extra-Propositional Aspects of Meaning (ExProM) in Computational Linguistics - NAACL '15*.

Ganitkevitch, J., Van Durme, B., and Callison-Burch, C. (2013). Ppdb: The paraphrase database. In *HLT-NAACL*, pages 758–764.

Gao, Q. and Vogel, S. (2008). Parallel implementations of word alignment tool. In *Software Engineering, Testing, and Quality Assurance for Natural Language Processing*, pages 49–57.

Germann, U., Jahr, M., Knight, K., Marcu, D., and Yamada, K. (2001). Fast decoding and optimal decoding for machine translation. In *Proceedings of the 39th Annual Meeting on Association for Computational Linguistics*, pages 228–235.

Hardmeier, C., Tiedemann, J., and Nivre, J. (2014). Translating pronouns with latent anaphora resolution. In *NIPS 2014 Workshop on Modern Machine Learning and Natural Language Processing*.

Koehn, P., Hoang, H., Birch, A., Callison-Burch, C., Federico, M., Bertoldi, N., Cowan, B., Shen, W., Moran, C., Zens, R., et al. (2007). Moses: Open source toolkit for statistical machine translation. In *Proceedings of the 45th annual meeting of the ACL on interactive poster and demonstration sessions*, pages 177–180.

Li, J.-J., Kim, J., Kim, D.-I., and Lee, J.-H. (2009). Chinese syntactic reordering for adequate generation of Korean verbal phrases in Chinese-to-Korean SMT. In *Proceedings of the Fourth Workshop on Statistical Machine Translation*, pages 190–196.

Li, X., Grimes, S., and Strassel, S. (2012). Gale chinese-english word alignment and tagging training part 3. Technical report, Philadelphia: Linguistic Data Consortium.

Manning, C. (2008). Generating typed dependency parses from phrase structure parses.

Morante, R. and Blanco, E. (2012). *SEM 2012 shared task: Resolving the scope and focus of negation. In *Proceedings of the First Joint Conference on Lexical and Computational Semantics-Volume 1: Proceedings of the main conference and the shared task, and Volume 2: Proceedings of the Sixth International Workshop on Semantic Evaluation*, pages 265–274.

Och, F. J. (2003). Minimum error rate training in statistical machine translation. In *Proceedings of the 41st Annual Meeting on Association for Computational Linguistics-Volume 1*, pages 160–167.

Read, J., Velldal, E., Øvrelid, L., and Oepen, S. (2012). Uio 1: constituent-based discriminative ranking for negation resolution. In *Proceedings of the First Joint Conference on Lexical and Computational Semantics-Volume 1: Proceedings of the main conference and the shared task, and Volume 2: Proceedings of the Sixth International Workshop on Semantic Evaluation*, pages 310–318.

Wetzel, D. and Bond, F. (2012). Enriching parallel corpora for statistical machine translation with semantic negation rephrasing. In *Proceedings of the Sixth Workshop on Syntax, Semantics and Structure in Statistical Translation*, pages 20–29.

Wisniewski, G. and Yvon, F. (2013). Oracle decoding as a new way to analyze phrase-based machine translation. *Machine translation*, 27(2):115–138.

Zhao, S., Lan, X., Liu, T., and Li, S. (2009). Application-driven statistical paraphrase generation. In *Proceedings of the Joint Conference of the 47th Annual Meeting of the ACL and the 4th International Joint Conference on Natural Language Processing of the AFNLP: Volume 2-Volume 2*, pages 834–842.

SMT error analysis and mapping to syntactic, semantic and structural fixes

Nora Aranberri
IXA Group
University of the Basque Country
Manuel Lardizabal 1, 20018 Donostia, Spain
nora.aranberri@ehu.eus

Abstract

This paper argues in favor of a linguistically-informed error classification for SMT to identify system weaknesses and map them to possible syntactic, semantic and structural fixes. We propose a scheme which includes both linguistic-oriented error categories as well as SMT-oriented edit errors, and evaluate an English-Spanish system and an English Basque system developed for a Q&A scenario in the IT domain. The classification, in our use-scenario, reveals great potential for fixes from lexical semantics techniques involving entity handling for IT-related names and user interface strings, word sense disambiguation for terminology, as well as argument structure for prepositions and syntactic parsing for various levels of reordering.

1 Introduction

Once we build a baseline SMT system, we run an evaluation to check its performance and guide improvement. Given the nature of statistical systems and their learning process, linguistic-oriented error analysis has been considered unfit for their evaluation. Even when it is identified that a particular linguistic feature is incorrectly handled, it is not clear how to specifically address it during training if we resort to common generic, non-deterministic techniques. However, when syntax, semantics and structure (SSS) come into play, error analysis regains relevance, as it can pinpoint specific aspects that can be addressed through the more targeted techniques they have brought to MT development.

Based on two baseline SMT systems, one for the English-Spanish pair and one for English-Basque, we present a methodology and classification for error analysis, a description of the results and a mapping to possible fixes using SSS techniques.

2 Error classification schemes

Different classification schemes have been proposed in the last years to categorize machine translation errors. Starting in the 90s, the LISA QA model was adopted by good part of the industry.[1] This model included a list of "objective" error types, graded by their severity and pre-assigned penalty points. The SAE J2450 standard, from the automotive service, also became popular.[2] What became clear from these first efforts was that no one-fits-all evaluation scheme is possible for MT. Each player within the translation workflow, from developers to vendors and clients, has its own needs and the information they expect from the evaluations is different.

After LISA ceased operations, two major efforts emerged: TAUS presented its Dynamic Quality Framework (DQF) [3] and the QTLaunchPad project developed the Multidimensional Quality Metrics (MQM).[4] The DQF tackles quality evaluation by identifying the objective of each evaluation and by offering a bundle of tools to satisfy each need. Specifically, they offer productivity testing based on post-editing effort, adequacy and fluency tests,

[1]The Localization Industry Standards Association terminated activities in 2011. No official reference is now available.
[2]SAE J2450: http://www.sae.org/standardsdev/j2450p1.htm
[3]DQF: https://evaluate.taus.net
[4]MQM: http://www.qt21.eu/mqm-definition

Proceedings of SSST-9, Ninth Workshop on Syntax, Semantics and Structure in Statistical Translation, pages 30–38,
Denver, Colorado, June 4, 2015.

translation comparisons and error classification. The error scheme, proposed after a thorough examination of industry practices, covers four main areas, namely, *Accuracy*, *Language*, *Terminology* and *Style*, with limited subcategories. With a strong industrial view, it focuses on establishing return-on-investment and on benchmarking performance to allow for informed decisions, rather than providing a detailed development-oriented error analysis.

The MQM is a framework that can be used to define metrics in order to assign a level of quality to a text. Each evaluation must identify the relevant categories for its goals and *customize* the metric. MQM Core is a hierarchy of 22 issues, at different levels of granularity. If we consider *Accuracy* and *Fluency*, the two top-level categories that best focus on intra-textual diagnosis, subcategories branch out and get more detailed, although they remain at a relatively general level. Authors claim that considerably more detailed subclasses might be necessary to diagnose MT problems and the framework allows for user-defined extensions, even if this is not encouraged.

The MQM puts together three different dimensions of error classification. The two top-level categories, *Accuracy* and *Fluency*, can be seen as the effect the errors have on a translated text. The concepts in the lower-levels include concepts of yet another two dimensions. Some of the subcategories refer to actual errors systems make, such as mistranslation or grammar, whereas others refer to the way in which these errors are rendered, namely, omission, addition and incorrect. When trying out the scheme to perform our evaluation, we saw that the distinction between fluency and accuracy might, to some extent, be useful when prioritizing fixes. However, we found difficulty in assigning an error to a specific subclass, as overlaps between dimensions occurred constantly. For example, grammar is placed under fluency but we could argue that an incorrect tense might lead to a significant change in meaning, and therefore, result in an accuracy issue. Similarly, one could claim that the rendering possibilities are true for almost, if not all, types of errors, rather than a category of their own. For example, Addition is a direct subclass of Accuracy, even if it is possible to find extra function words in a translation. Also, we strongly felt that some subclasses were too broad to be meaningful to decide on a targeted SSS solution.

Among schemes that have emerged from research groups, Vilar et al. (2006) presented one of the first to focus on identifying errors made by statistical systems. Probably motivated by the fact that these systems are not controlled by linguistic rules and are not deterministic in this respect, the top-level categories proposed were *Missing words*, *Word order*, *Incorrect words*, *Unknown words* and *Punctuation*, that is, types of edits unrelated to linguistic reasoning. The lower categories are slightly more linguistic but they remain on SMT parameters such as *local/long range*, *stems* and *forms*. While *Word order* and *Unknown words* point to specific efforts for improvement, the *Incorrect words* category is broad and requires, as the authors suggest, further customization depending on the language pair at hand. Again, this classification lacks the linguistic detail we aimed to collect for linguistically-oriented fixes.

2.1 Classification schemes: our approach

Given our goal and the nature of our systems, we opted for a general linguistic classification with an additional dimension to cover the edit type of each error: missing, additional or incorrect (Figure 1). Once a linguistic error is identified, it is classified based on the edit-type dimension. We established six top-level linguistic categories, which are further detailed in subclasses. These subclasses are not static but rather they can be omitted or extended during evaluation to suit errors found in texts. The linguistic depth and the clear division between dimensions overcomes the lack of detail of the DQF model and the overlaps that emerged in the MQM model, while incorporating the SMT-oriented edits proposed by Vilar et al. (2006).

We worked with a two-to-four-level scheme to gather as much detail as possible about the errors found. We describe the six main categories below.

Top-level category	Subclasses	Incorrect	Missing	Additional
Lexis				
Morphosyntax				
Verbs				
Order				
Punctuation				
Untranslated				

Figure 1: Proposed bidimensional error scheme.

1. Lexis

   This category includes incorrect choices for general vocabulary and terminology, as well as longer set phrases, idioms or expressions.

2. Morphosyntax

   This category includes morphological and syntactic errors. We fused both categories as these types of errors are often so intertwined that it is difficult to opt for one category over the other. Moreover, the classification is proposed as a tool to easily summarize and assimilate system error information and the exact top-level classification of the items should not have an impact on research decisions. This should be guided by their fixing requirements and possibilities.

3. Verbs

   A separate category was defined for verb phrases because of their complexity. Whereas English verb phrases carry lexical, aspectual, tense, modality and voice information, Spanish verb phrases also have subject information, and in the case of Basque, information about objects is also included. The high variability of conjugated verbs and auxiliaries poses great difficulty for statistical systems. We divided this category into subgroups based on the information mentioned above.

4. Order

   Again, this is a dedicated category due to the impact order has on the overall comprehensibility of the translations and because it is a property that can be addressed specifically in statistical systems. We distinguished several levels: sentence, clause and phrase. Also, we identify whether the issues involve orderings of units of the same level or, unit-specific issues, which can be internal orderings or splits.

5. Punctuation

   This category includes punctuation and orthographic issues such as punctuation marks, capitalization and orthotactic constrains (orthographic rules governing lemma-affix gluing).

6. Untranslated

   We added a category for source words that are left in the original language.

3 The systems

3.1 English-Spanish

The English-Spanish system is a standard phrase-based system built on Moses (Koehn, et al. 2007). It uses basic tokenization and a pattern excluding URLs, truecasing and language model interpolation. It has been trained on bilingual corpora including Europarl, United Nations, News Commentary and Common Crawl ($\sim$355 million words). The monolingual corpora used to learn the language model include the Spanish texts of Europarl, News Commentary and News Crawl ($\sim$60 million words). For tuning, a set of 1,000 in-domain interactions (question-answer pairs) were made available. The original interactions are in English and they were translated into Spanish by human translators.

The system was evaluated on a test-set similar to that used for tuning: a second batch of 1,000 in-domain interactions. The English-Spanish system obtains a BLEU score of 45.86.

3.2 English-Basque

The English-Basque system is also a standard phrase-based system built on Moses. It uses basic tokenization, lemmatization and lowercasing. Stanford CoreNLP (Manning et al., 2014) is used for English analysis and Eustagger (Alegría et al., 2002) for Basque. It uses a 5-gram language model. To better address the agglutinative nature of Basque, the word alignments were obtained over the lemmas, and were then projected to the original word forms to complete the training process.

The system was trained on translation memory (TM) data containing academic books, software manuals and user interface strings ($\sim$12 million words), and web-crawled data ($\sim$1.5 million words) made available by Elhuyar.[5] For the language model, the Basque text of the parallel data and the Basque text of Spanish-Basque TMs of administrative text made available by Elhuyar ($\sim$7.4 million sentences) was used. Again, a set of 1,000 in-domain interactions were used for tuning after manually translating the original text into Basque.

The system was evaluated on a second test-set of 1,000 in-domain interactions, obtaining a BLEU score of 20.24.

[5] Elhuyar: https://www.elhuyar.eus/en

Error category	Examples
lexis	Click *run* where it says vulnerabilities. Pulse *correr* donde dice vulnerabilidades. (run=sport)
morphosyntax	Yes, you can share files and folders with one or more users *on MEO* Cloud. Sí, puede compartir archivos y carpetas con uno o más usuarios *sobre* MEO Cloud. (on=about)
verb	*Connect* your computer to the ZON HUB via Ethernet cable. *Conectar* su ordenador a la HUB af a travs de cable Ethernet. (to connect)
ordering	Tap "Import" to copy your *Android browser favorites*. Toca "Importar" para copiar su *navegador de Android favoritos*. (~your favorites Android browser)
punctuation	If I buy a computer abroad, will it work in Portugal Si compro un ordenador en el extranjero, funcionará en Portugal*?* (missing ¿)
untranslated	*Then* click on the yellow disc with a green tick. *Then* haga clic en el disco de color amarillo con una marca verde.

Table 1: Examples of errors per top-level category for the English-Spanish pair.

4 Error analysis results [6]

4.1 Error analysis for the English-Spanish pair

We randomly selected 100 interventions (questions or answers) included in the use-scenario test set. Overall, out of 137 sentences (each intervention might consist of several sentences) 30 sentences were found to be correct, and the remaining 107 include 169 errors, at least 3 errors per intervention.

Lexical errors account for 31% of the total mistakes (see examples for top-level categories in Table 1). Around half emerge from the translation of user interface (UI) strings. Although it was not possible to identify whether the translations matched the final software version text exactly, in some cases the translations are clearly awkward. Problems are most relevant in multi-word strings, which are not translated as a unit, resulting in partial translations and inadequate capitalization. The translations of software and brand names display a similar behavior. These proper names tend to stay the same across languages, but the system does not always treat them this way. Adding to this, multiword names often get part of the name translated.

Issues with general vocabulary and terminology (we will consider terminology words that acquire a specialized meaning in our domain or words that are specific to our domain) are also present. Whereas some inadequate translations do not have a clear origin, a good number of them clearly emerge from incorrect word sense disambiguation.

Morphosyntactic errors account for about 29% of the total errors. Although they are very widespread across the different subcategories, we find that prepositions, subordinate markers and POS errors are the most recurrent cases.

[6]For a complete classification see appendices A and B.

The Verbs category accounts for 18% of the errors. Although a number of verbs lack the correct agreement or use an inadequate tense or voice, the most recurrent error seems to come from the mode. This is typical of instructional texts, where orders, given with the infinitive form in English can be translated as imperatives or infinitives. This is usually a stylistic decision but one that needs to be consistent across the documentation and, in particular, within the sentence or paragraph.

A number of order issues have been identified (11%), which mainly involve the composition of multiword noun phrases. We found 7 cases where a noun phrase was split and 7 cases where the elements were incorrectly ordered despite staying in close proximity.

Punctuation errors (6%) and untranslated words (5%) are low. The former include cases of incorrect capitalization and use of question-initial marks. The latter involve function and content words.

4.2 Error analysis for the English-Basque pair

We again performed a random selection of 100 interventions. Based on overall counts, 6 out of 140 sentences were correct and the remaining 134 included 393 errors, at least 7 errors per intervention.

Lexical errors account for around 23% of the total (Table 2). Despite a number of errors due to incorrect word sense disambiguation, most errors emerge from UI strings and software/brand name translations. Capitalization errors in these units were included in this subcategory (36 cases).

Morphosyntactical errors account for over 39%

Error category	Examples
lexis	Go to WhatsApp > *"Menu Button"* > "Status". Joan *menu botoia* WhatsApp > " " > " egoera ". (unrecognized user interface path)
morphosyntax	Yes it is possible, simply by dragging the profile of the person concerned *to* the various circles. Bai posible da, besterik gabe, arrastatu pertsonaren profila hainbat nahia zirkulu. (missing postposition for circles-zirkulu)
verb	Choose a standard status or personalize one. Egoera estandar bat edo pertsonalizatu bat. (missing verb choose)
ordering	*You can use the app iPP Podcast Player* you find on Google Play. *Aplikazioa erabil dezakezu IPP podcast Player* aurkitu duzu Google erreproduzitu. (The app you can use IPP podcast Player...)
punctuation	How can I change the language to of Mega to Portuguese? Nola aldatu hizkuntza of Mega, portugesa? (additional comma)
untranslated	How much space do I have for free *on* Mega? Zenbat leku ditut doan *on* Mega?

Table 2: Examples of errors per top-level category for the English-Basque pair.

of the total errors. Most, around 64%, concern the translation of prepositions and subordinate conjunctions. In Basque, prepositions are translated into postpositions that are attached to the last word of the phrase (the nucleus) and the same happens with subordinate markers, attached to the last word of the subordinate clause. It is worth noting the high number of missing elements in this subcategory, 90 cases recorded out of 149 (10 cases out of 49 for Spanish).

Verbs show a considerable number of errors (18%), specially if we take into account that 21 main verbs, which display the lexical meaning and the aspect, and 23 auxiliaries, which display tense, mode and paradigm, are missing. Out of the verb phrases that are constructed, the aspect, the paradigm and agreements generate errors.

Order errors account for 14% of the total errors. The sequencing of noun phrase elements stands out as the main source of errors, whether within the phrase or because splits occurred. The positioning of relative clauses with respect to their heads also emerged as a problematic area with 11 occurrences.

Punctuation (4%) and untranslated words (1%) are low, the most salient being missing commas.

4.3 Fixing possibilities with syntax, semantics and structure

From the error analysis of the English-Spanish and English-Basque systems we see that errors emerge from two main sources, use-scenario-specific features and language pair-specific features.

The text-type and domain of the translations has an impact on the difficulties the system encounters. In the case we present, we work on a question-and-answer (Q&A) scenario in the information technology (IT) domain. The texts, therefore, mainly consist of instructions and descriptions, and include a high degree of terminology, brand and software names, as well as UI strings. And our systems have difficulty in dealing with them.

Lexical semantics, and in particular, (cross-lingual) named-entity recognition (NER) and translation techniques could greatly benefit our application scenario. Following the implementation of NER in MT by Li et al. (2013), Li et al. (2012) and similar, it would be possible to train a NER system to identify IT names. We could possibly create a separate category for the disambiguation process (NED) if we envisage to treat them in a specific way. For example, we may decide that NEs classified as *IT-name* should be left in English, or that they should be looked up in Wikipedia following techniques such as Mihalcea and Csomai's (2007) and Agirre et al.'s (2015) to find an equivalent entry in the target language, and as a result, its translation. Maybe we could opt for dynamic searches in multilingual websites of specific brands or the use of pre-compiled dictionaries from these resources.

The NER system could be expanded to include UIs. Cues to identify them could be anchors like *icon, tab* and *dialog box*, and phrases such as *where it says*, and > sequences. The systems had difficulty in identifying UIs and often provided translations that differ significantly from the strings we are used to seeing in software graphics. UIs usually have a fixed translation - often given by the product-maker - and they must be treated as proper nouns in the sense that they are usually capitalized (first word only if multiword) and do not accept articles. We could chose to identify them and translate them using a specialized dictionary or even let the MT system output a candidate which considers the restrictions just mentioned.

Sense disambiguation, whether for general words or terms, has also been identified as a category worth addressing. Word sense disambiguation techniques along the line of Carpuat et al. (2013), for example, could help. They propose a technique to identify unknown senses to the system, most probably because they are domain-specific senses not covered by the training corpus. Once marked, we could divert them and translate them using a specialised resource.

Out of the language pair-specific errors, the most glaring are Basque postpositional renderings of English prepositions. Predicate-argument structures and semantic roles, as suggested by the work of Liu and Gildea (2010) and Kawahara and Kurohashi (2010), are a way to improve the incorrect renderings and to force missing postpositions. Resources such as the Basque Verb Index (BVI) (Estarrona et al., forthcoming), which includes Basque verb subcategorization based on PropBank and VerbNet, with syntactic renderings assigned to each argument and mappings to WordNet for crosslingual information, can be a starting point in this task.

Order errors have shown three types of issues: (i) phrases or chunks ordered incorrectly; (ii) phrases split along the sentence; and (iii) phrasal elements kept local but with incorrect phrase-internal order. For the first case, semantics has proposed the use of argument structure to learn reordering patterns (Wu et al., 2011). For cases ii and iii, syntax would have to come into play. Firstly, we need to provide the MT with phrase boundary information so that contiguous phrases are not mixed. Secondly, phrase-internal reordering patterns or restrictions need to apply. Yeniterzi and Oflazer (2010), for example, encode a variety of local and non-local syntactic structures of the source side as complex structural tags and include this information as additional factors during training. Also, working on POS, Popović and Ney (2006) propose source-side local reordering patterns for Spanish-English and, working on syntactic parse-level, Wang et al. (2007) propose reordering patterns to address systematic differences (Chinese-English). Xiong et al. (2010) go beyond syntax and propose translation zones as unit boundaries, improving constituent-based approaches.

We finally focus on the generation of verb phrases, particularly relevant for the English-Basque pair, where verbs tend to go missing, but also to remedy incorrect verbal features in both pairs. The sparsity due to the complexity and morphological variety of Spanish and, even more so, Basque verb phrases is most probably the main reason for their incorrect handling. This leads us to proposing the generalization of features, such as lemmatization of verbs, while suggesting a parallel transfer of source verb features to final postprocessing, for instance. Work on verbal transfer has not received attention so far, unless integrated within argument structure techniques, such as the work of Xiong et al. (2012).

5 Conclusions

We proposed a dynamic, extensible linguistically-informed error classification for SMT which includes six top-level linguistic error categories with further subclasses, and a second dimension for SMT-oriented edits covering additions, omissions and incorrect words. This addresses the lack of linguistic detail and flexibility of metrics such as the DQF, and integrates the SMT-oriented errors proposed by Vilar et al. (2006) avoiding overlaps found in MQM.

We evaluated an English-Spanish and an English-Basque system developed for a Q&A scenario in the IT domain. The classification revealed issues strongly related to the domain and more general language pair-specific errors. We identified terminology and UI strings as the main issue for the lexical category. The morphosyntactic category showed more diverging issues. The most striking was the weak handling of English prepositions, and in particular, the poor generation of Basque postpositions, governing English prepositions and subordinate markers. The complexity of target-side verbs also took its toll on system performance with incorrect features for Spanish and an alarming number of missing main verbs and auxiliaries for Basque. As expected, ordering errors occurred at all levels, internal and external. Punctuation and Untranslated showed a low number of errors.

The exercise served to link the potential relevance of syntax, semantics and structure to fix language-specific SMT errors and the suitability of lexical semantics for IT-domain terminology and UI strings.

Acknowledgments

The research leading to these results has received funding from FP7-ICT-2013-10-610516 (QTLeap).

References

Eneko Agirre, Ander Barrena and Aitor Soroa. 2015. *Studying the Wikipedia Hyperlink Graph for Relatedness and Disambiguation.* arXiv:1503.01655.

Iñaki Alegría, María Jesús Aranzabe, Anton Ezeiza, Nerea Ezeiza and Ruben Urizar. 2002. *Robustness and customisation in an analyser/lemmatiser for Basque.* Proceedings of the LREC-2002 Workshop on Customizing knowledge in NLP applications.

Marine Carpuat, Hal Daumé III, Katharine Henry, Ann Irvine, Jagadeesh Jagarlamudi and Rachel Rudinger. 2013. *Studying the Wikipedia Hyperlink Graph for Relatedness and Disambiguation.* Proceedings of the 51st Annual Meeting of the Association for Computational Linguistics, Sofia, Bulgaria, pages 1435–1445.

Ainara Estarrona, Izaskun Aldezabal, Aranza Díaz de Ilarraza and María Jesús Aranzabe. Forthcoming. *Methodology of construction of the corpus-based Basque Verb Index (BVI) Lexicon* Language Resources and Evaluation.

Daisuke Kawahara and Sadao Kurohashi. 2010. *Acquiring Reliable Predicate-argument Structures from Raw Corpora for Case Frame Compilation* Proceedings of the Seventh International Conference on Language Resources and Evaluation (LREC'10), Valleta, Malta, pages 1389–1393.

Philipp Koehn, Hieu Hoang, Alexandra Birch, Chris Callison-Burch, Marcello Federico, Nicola Bertoldi, Brooke Cowan, Wade Shen, Christine Moran, Richard Zens, Chris Dyer, Ondej Bojar, Alexandra Constantin, Evan Herbst. 2007. *AMoses: open source toolkit for statistical machine translation.* Proceedings of the 45th Annual Meeting of the ACL on Interactive Poster and Demonstration Sessions, Prague, Czech Republic.

Qi Li, Haibo Li, Heng Ji, Wen Wang, Jing Zheng and Fei Huang. 2012. *Joint Bilingual Name Tagging for Parallel Corpora.* In Proceeding of CIKM12, pages 1727–1731.

Haibo Li, Jing Zheng, Heng Ji, Qi Li and Wen Wang. 2013. *Name-aware Machine Translation* Proceedings of the 51st Annual Meeting of the Association for Computational Linguistics, Sofia, Bulgaria, pages 604–614.

Ding Liu and Daniel Gildea. 2010. *Semantic role features for machine translation* Proceedings of the 23rd International Conference on Computational Linguistics, pages 716–724.

Christopher Manning, Mihai Surdeanu, John Bauer, Jenny Finkel, Steven Bethard and David McClosky. 2014. *The Stanford CoreNLP Natural Language Processing Toolkit.* In Proceedings of 52nd Annual Meeting of the Association for Computational Linguistics: System Demonstrations, pages 55–60.

Rada Mihalcea and Andras Csomai. 2007. *SenseSpotting: Never let your parallel data tie you to an old domain.* In Proceedings of the sixteenth ACM conference on Conference on information and knowledge management, pages 233–242. ACM.

Maja Popović and Hermann Ney. 2006. *POS-based Word Reorderings for Statistical Machine Translation.* Proceedings on the fifth international conference on Language Resources and Evaluation, LREC 2006, Genoa, Italy, pages 1278–1283.

David Vilar, Jia Xu, Luis Fernando DHaro and Hermann Ney. 2006. *Error Analysis of Statistical Machine Translation Output.* Proceedings on the fifth international conference on Language Resources and Evaluation, LREC 2006, Genoa, Italy, pages 697–702.

Chao Wang, Michael Collins and Philipp Koehn. 2007. *Chinese Syntactic Reordering for Statistical Machine Translation.* Proceedings of the 2007 Joint Conference on Empirical Methods in Natural Language Processing and Computational Natural Language Learning, Prague, pages 737745.

Xianchao Wu, Katsuhito Sudoh, Kevin Duh, Hajime Tsukada, Masaaki Nagata. 2011. *Extracting Preordering Rules from Predicate-Argument Structures.* Proceedings of the 5th International Joint Conference on Natural Language Processing, Chiang Mai, Thailand, pages 29–37.

Deyi Xiong, Min Zhang and Haizhou Li. 2012. *Verb Translation and Argument Reordering.* Proceedings of the 48th Annual Meeting of the Association for Computational Linguistics, Uppsala, Sweden, pages 902–911.

Deyi Xiong, Min Zhang and Haizhou Li. 2010. *Learning Translation Boundaries for Phrase-based Decoding.* Proceedings of the 2010 Annual Conference of the North American Chapter of the ACL, Los Angeles, California, pages 136–144.

Reyyan Yeniterzi and Kemal Oflazer. 2010. *Syntax-to-Morphology Mapping in Factored Phrase-Based Statistical Machine Translation from English to Turkish* Proceedings of the 48th Annual Meeting of the Association for Computational Linguistics, Uppsala, Sweden, pages 454–464.

A Error classification scheme and results for the English-Spanish pair

Main category	Subcategory 1	Subcategory 2	Incorrect	Missing	Additional
Lexis (53)	Vocabulary	lexical choice	2 (53)		
		sense	6		
	Terminology	lexical choice	4		
		sense	6		
	software brand names		8		
	UI issues		27		
Morphosyntax (49)	POS		9 (31)	(10)	(8)
	preposition		7	1	3
	noun			1	2
	adjective	agreement	2		
	determiner	other		3	
		agreement	1		
	article				2
	pronoun	other	1		
		gender	1		
		formal vs informal	3		
	interrogative pronoun		3		
	attribute	other	1		
		agreement		1	
	coordinator				1
	subordinate markers	relative marker	1	2	
		completive marker		2	
		purpose marker	1		
	coreference	agreement	1		
Verbs (30)	verb phrase		2 (26)	(4)	
	subject agreement		1	2	
	tense		2	1	
	mode	other		1	
		disagreement	7		
		infinite vs imperative	9		
	voice	passive	3		
	auxiliary		2		
Order (19)	noun phrase - internal		9 (19)		
	split noun phrase		7		
	split prepositional phrase		1		
	verb-adverb		2		
Punctuation (10)	capitalization	uppercase	4 (4)	(5)	(1)
	accent			1	
	question mark			4	1
Untranslated (8)			8 (8)		
Total (169)			141	19	9

B Error classification scheme and results for the English-Basque pair

Main category	Subcategory 1	Subcategory 2	Incorrect		Missing		Additional	
		lexical choice	3	(93)				
	Vocabulary	sense	3					
Lexis (93)	Terminology	sense	4					
	software brand names		28					
	UI issues		55					
	POS		11	(51)		(90)		(11)
	preposition		23		43		2	
	noun	other			1			
		agreement	3					
	adjective			2	2		1	
	determiner				1		1	
	article		5		1			
	adverb				5			
	pronoun				1			
	interrogative pronoun		1		7		1	
	negation (verbs)				1		2	
Morphosyntax (154)	coordinator						1	
	coordinated subclause		5		4			
	superlative structure		2					
		relative marker			11			
		relative marker			3		1	
		completive marker			3			
	subordinate markers	purpose marker	1		4		2	
		reason marker			1			
		temporal marker			1			
		conditional marker			1			
	verb phrase		4	(19)		(45)	2	(2)
	main verb					21		
	auxiliary verb					23		
	subject agreement			3				
Verbs (70)	direct object agreement			2				
	tense			1				
	aspect		5					
	auxiliary			4		1		
	paradigm			4				
	constituent-level		2	(55)				
	noun phrase - internal		19					
Order (55)	split noun phrase		7					
	split prepositional phrase		3					
	clause-level		1					
	clause internal		2					
	clause split		1					
	head-relative clause		11					
	contiguous sentences merged		9					
Punctuation (16)	capitalization		2	(4)		(11)		(1)
	comma		2		11			
	EOS						1	
Untranslated (5)			5	(5)				
Total (393)				233		135		25

Unsupervised False Friend Disambiguation Using Contextual Word Clusters and Parallel Word Alignments

Maryam Aminian, Mahmoud Ghoneim, Mona Diab
Department of Computer Science
The George Washington University
Washington, DC
{aminian,mghoneim,mtdiab}@gwu.edu

Abstract

Lexical false friends (FF) are the phenomena where words that look the same, do not have the same meaning or lexical usage. FF impose several challenges to statistical machine translation. We present a methodology which exploits word context modeling as well as information provided by word alignments for identifying false friends and choosing the right sense for them in the context. We show that our approach enhances SMT lexical choice for false friends across language variants. We demonstrate that our approach reduces word error rate (WER) and position independent error rate (PER) for Egyptian-English SMT by 0.6% and 0.1% compared to the baseline.

1 Introduction

False friends (FF), aka faux amis, are words in two or more language variants that are orthographically and/or phonetically similar but do not convey the same meaning (Brown and Allan, 2010). FF sense divergence is one of the main sources of performance degradation in statistical machine translation (SMT) systems. These words are frequently observed when the underlying distribution of the test set is different from that of the train data. In other words, the sense of a particular word in the input sentence varies from all observed senses of that word in the train data. Thus, SMT may choose the target language translation which is considered inappropriate based on the context.

Standard form of a language has different informal spoken varieties which are known as dialects. For instance, standard form of Arabic has different dialects (Habash, 2010). These dialects typically share a set of cognates that could bear the same meaning in both varieties or only be shared homographs but serve as false friend. The usage of dialects in textual social media and communication channels is rapidly increasing. On the other hand, usually there is not enough dialectal parallel data to train the translation model and build stand alone machine translation systems for dialects. However, the standard official forms of language usually have a wealth of resources and tools that can be adapted to dialects of that language.

The main goal of this paper is to enhance dialectal SMT performance without any in-domain training data. We move towards this goal by performing a pre-processing phase which includes, 1) identifying false friends in the input sentence and, 2) replacing them with an appropriate equivalent from standard language which bears the same meaning. By doing this, we benefit from availability of standard parallel data to choose a more accurate target translation for the false friends.

We aim to identify false friends without any labeled training data. We then try to choose equivalents from the standard language for the identified false friends. We exploit a classifier for identifying false friends and designing a word sense disambiguator for finding the best equivalent from the standard language. We employ unsupervised word alignment from parallel text and a taxonomy-based semantic similarity measure (Wu and Palmer, 1994) to automatically acquire training data for the FF identifier. Our word sense disambiguator benefits from unsupervised word clusters to model the context. We obtain word clusters from a large monolingual text in the standard language. Training the model only involves counting the coocurrences of

Proceedings of SSST-9, Ninth Workshop on Syntax, Semantics and Structure in Statistical Translation, pages 39–48,
Denver, Colorado, June 4, 2015.

each word with word clusters for different context definitions. During decoding (disambiguation), for a word in a sentence, we estimate the likelihood for each equivalent of that word given word clusters in its surrounding context.

We evaluate our method on Egyptian (EGY) to English (EN) SMT using a translation model trained on Modern Standard Arabic (MSA). We show that our approach improves EGY-to-EN SMT lexical choice and reachs 0.6% and 0.1% reduction in word error rate (WER) and position-independent error (PER) (Tillmann et al., 1997) over the baseline respectively. In summary, the main contributions of this paper are: 1) designing a FF identifier with a supervised classifier trained on automatically acquired labeled data, 2) designing a disambiguator for replacing FF with their equivalent standard form and 3) improving the SMT lexical choice on dialectal data without using any in-domain parallel data to train SMT model.

The remainder of this paper is organized as follows: We give a literature overview in §2. We then detail our approach in §3 . We present t experiments in §4 and discuss the results in §5. We finally make conclusions in §6.

2 Related Work

There have been several studies for identifying false friends which benefit from parallel data to measure semantic similarity of words (Frunza and Inkpen, 2006; Nakov et al., 2009; Inkpen et al., 2005; Kondrak, 2001; Mitkov et al., 2007). Some other studies such as (Nakov et al., 2007; Schulz et al., 2004; Nakov et al., 2009; Mulloni et al., 2007) exploit distributional semantics to identify false friends. These methods hypothesize that words occurring in similar contexts tend to be semantically similar. Methods leveraging this idea usually use vector space models to show the local context of the target word. Context can be modeled either with a window of a certain size around the target word e.g. (Nakov et al., 2009) and (Schulz et al., 2004) or words in a particular syntactic relationships with the target word e.g. (Mulloni et al., 2007).

The most comparable work to our false friend identification approach is the work done by Mitkov et al. (2007) which uses both distributional semantic evidences extracted from monolingual data and bilingual hints obtained from comparable corpora. They eventually use this information as features in a false friend classifier and reach up to 20% and 37% improvement over the baseline precision and recall respectively. Our false friend identification method is different from the mentioned studies in the sense that we generate a supervised classifier from fully unsupervised labeled data. Unlike previous work that solely focus on the identification task, our model leverages both identification and disambiguation.

From the sense disambiguation perspective, there have been several attempts to integrate word sense disambiguation (WSD) systems into the SMT framework in recent years. The main goal of these studies is to improve the target translation for an ambiguous word in the source sentence. Most studies in this area incorporate supervised WSD systems which exploit labeled training data. As an instance, Carpuat and Wu (Carpuat and Wu, 2005) integrate a supervised WSD model trained on the Senseval-3 Chinese lexical sample task data into a standard Chinese-English phrase-based SMT model with two methodologies: First, at the decode time, they limit set of translation candidates for an ambiguous word to the set of translations mapped to the sense predicted by the WSD model. Second, they replace the translations chosen by SMT with the translation predicted by WSD system. Nevertheless, they show none of these methods improves baseline BLEU score (Papineni et al., 2002). Vickrey et al (2005) formulate the task of using WSD for SMT as *word translation* task. They use parallel data to train their WSD model. They showed that they improve accuracy in both word translation and blank-filling tasks. However, they did not incorporate their word translation setup in an end-to-end SMT system.

Carpuat and Wu (2007) transformed the problem into a phrase sense disambiguation task by incorporating state-of-the-art WSD features for selecting a target phrase out of all aligned phrases as the possible senses. Chan et al (2007) also embedded state-of-the-art WSD system into SMT by adding more features into the SMT model. They showed that they improve Baseline BLEU score using their WSD-based model.

Yang and Kirchhoff (2012) use an unsupervised

WSD to improve SMT final performance. Similar to previous studies, they add the WSD acquired feature to the SMT model. They could improve the BLEU score by 0.3% compared to the baseline.

All the mentioned studies aim to enhance SMT by identifying the appropriate target translation for a source word in a given context. Our approach is different from previous work in two aspects: First, we try to improve SMT lexical choice by identifying false friends and replacing them with the most adequate equivalent from standard language. Unlike previous work, all these steps are done on a given input sentence and we can see them as a preprocessing phase, thereby, there is no need to change the SMT model. Second, our approach does not assume that the in-domain parallel data is available. Hence, it is not constrained by the domain and can be extended to any other language variants.

The main difference between this approach and our previous work as described in (Aminian et al., 2014) lies in the fact that we try to improve SMT lexical choice by enhancing FF translation. Rather than blindly replacing all dialectal words with their standard equivalent as we did in (Aminian et al., 2014), here we try to automatically identify FF as one of the important sources of translation degradation across language variants and leverage knowledge acquired from monolingual standard data to predict the best equivalent for FF based on the context.

3 Approach

We describe our model in this section. We use two modules in our model: 1) a FF identifier (henceforth PARL) and, 2) a disambiguator (henceforth WC). PARL is based on a supervised classifier. The training data for PARL is automatically obtained from parallel data. WC is based on the likelihood of each standard equivalent given the contextual information. In all of our definitions, we use DA and ST to refer to a dialectal and standard language, respectively.

3.1 PARL Classifier

We first give some basic definitions about the setup. Parallel text $\mathcal{D}$ is a set of aligned sentences $\mathcal{S} = \{\mathcal{S}_1, \mathcal{S}_2, ..., \mathcal{S}_N\}$ and $\mathcal{S}' = \{\mathcal{S}'_1, \mathcal{S}'_2, ..., \mathcal{S}'_N\}$ in the source and target languages respectively. We assume $\mathcal{S}'$ to be English (EN) in our experiments. $\mathcal{S}$ contains both ST and DA sentences. Each training instance is shown with a tuple (k, i, y) in which $1 \leq k \leq |\mathcal{S}|$, $1 \leq i \leq |\mathcal{S}_k|$ and $y \in \mathcal{Y}$. $\mathcal{Y}$ refers to the set of labels $\{$FF, NFF$\}$. We represent the ith word in the kth sentence as w_{ki} and its features as $\phi(k, i) \in \mathbb{R}^d$ where d is the size of feature vector. Given the set of training tuples (k, i, y), a classification algorithm is used to train the model. We use Averaged Perceptron (Freund and Schapire, 1999) as our classifier with the following features: word form for the current word and part of speech tag for the previous, current and next words.

Automatic Label Estimation We use a dialect identification tool to define a function $\mathcal{L}(k, i)$, that identifies the dialect for w_{ki} out of two possibilities: DA and ST. We do word alignment on $\mathcal{D}$ using an unsupervised alignment algorithm. We define A_{ki} to be the English word aligned to w_{ki}. Accordingly, we define E_w^{ST} as the set of all English words aligned to the source word w for the cases where w is identified as ST. E_w^{ST} can be written as:

$$E_w^{ST} = \{\forall e \in EN | \exists j, h \; A_{j,h} = e, \; w_{j,h} = w, \; \mathcal{L}(j, h) = ST\} \quad (1)$$

To reduce noise in the automatically acquired word alignments, we just consider aligned word pairs with frequency more than 5. For each w_{ki} where $\mathcal{L}(k, i)$ is equal to DA, we have to decide whether the word is FF or not. We define a function $\mathcal{F}(w_{ki}, A_{ki})$ that returns true if we decide to label w_{ki} as FF and false otherwise (Eq. 2).

$$\mathcal{F}(w_{ki}, A_{ki}) = true \Leftrightarrow Sim(A_{ki}, E_{w_{ki}}^{ST}) < \delta \quad (2)$$

where δ is a manually defined threshold and Sim is defined in Eq. 3:

$$Sim(e, E) = \frac{1}{|\mathcal{C}_E|} \sum_{c \in \mathcal{C}_E} \frac{\sum_{e' \in c} dist(e, e')}{|c|} \quad (3)$$

where $\mathcal{C}_E$ partitions E into non-overlapping clusters. Each $c \in \mathcal{C}_E$ contains a cluster of words in E with similar meaning. The clusters are obtained from using the distance measure (Wu and Palmer, 1994) in Eq. 4.

$$dist(e, e') = \frac{2 \cdot d(s_{e,e'})}{d(e) + d(e')} \quad (4)$$

where $s_{e,e'}$ is a maximally specific superclass of e and e' in WordNet (Miller, 1995) and d is the depth of the node in the WordNet taxonomy.

In short, Eq. 3 computes a weighted average similarity between various ST senses of the target word and its DA sense in the sentence k. The intuition behind this setting is as follows: for a particular word that is identified as DA in a sentence, we measure similarity of its aligned English word to the set of all English words aligned to ST occurrences of the same word (E_w^{ST}). If this similarity is less than a threshold δ, we label that word as FF. We set δ to 0.5 in our experiments.

3.2 WC Classifier

We now describe our disambiguation model. We use a large amount of monolingual data $\mathcal{D}'$ as a set of sentences $\mathcal{S} = \{\mathcal{S}_1, \mathcal{S}_2, ..., \mathcal{S}_M\}$ in the ST form. We perform unsupervised word clustering on $\mathcal{D}'$ to obtain word cluster assignments for each word. We then use word clusters to build our disambiguation model. The model comprises five parameters: $P_{-2}(c|w)$, $P_{-1}(c|w)$, $P_{+1}(c|w)$ and $P_{+2}(c|w)$ for all $c \in \{1, 2, ..., K\}$ where K refers to the number of clusters, in addition to the word probability $P(w)$. Hence, context parameters are $P_\tau(c|w)$ for $\tau \in \{-2, -1, +1, +2\}$ in which c specifies cluster of the word which is placed in the offset τ for the word w. $P_\tau(c|w)$ is estimated using maximum likelihood estimation with additive smoothing. The smoothing parameter is set to 0.1 in our experiments. To avoid sparsity, we assume that all previous contexts are the same and analogously all next contexts are also the same. In other words, we tie $P_{-2}(c|w)$ and $P_{-1}(c|w)$ into one parameter and $P_2(c|w)$ and $P_1(c|w)$ into another distinct parameter.

Let $\Omega(w)$ be the list of ST equivalents for the DA word w. We choose the most probable candidate ω^* using Eq. 5 by having $\tau \in \{-2, -1, 1, 2\}$.

$$\omega^* = \underset{\omega \in \Omega}{\text{argmax}} \; \log P(\omega) + \sum_{\tau} \log P_\tau(c_\tau|\omega) \quad (5)$$

The intuition behind this model is as follows: if a particular DA word in a sentence is identified as FF, we want to replace it by one of its ST equivalents. If an alternative word is more likely to appear in that context compared to other possible equivalents, we expect our model to select that as the replacement. Since we train word clusters on ST data, the model tends to assign more weight on words that fit better to ST contexts.

4 Experimental Setup

Data Sets To train PARL classifier, we use parallel data $\mathcal{D}_{ME}$ which is a collection of MSA and EGY texts created from multiple LDC catalogs.[1] The data comprises 29M MSA and 5M DA tokenized words from multiple genres including newswire, broadcast news, broadcast conversations, and weblogs. To train the disambiguator, we use the Arabic Gigaword 4 (Graff and Cieri, 2003) containing 848M tokenized MSA words. To train the model described in § 3.2, we exclude punctuation as well as clitics from the target word local context. These words usually do not provide much information about the target word and will increase model sparsity. All data sets used in our experiments have undergone the following preprocessing steps: all Arabic data is Alef/Ya normalized and tokenized using MADAMIRA v1. (Pasha et al., 2014) according to Arabic Treebank (ATB) tokenization scheme (Maamouri et al., 2004). We used Tree Tagger (Schmid, 1994) to tokenize English data.

Tools We use GIZA++ (Och and Ney, 2003) for word alignment. We obtain word clusters from word2vec (Mikolov et al., 2013) K-means word clustering tool. We use the continuous bag of word model to build word vectors of size 200 using a word window of size 8 for both left and right. The number of negative samples for logistic regression is set to 25 and threshold used for sub-sampling of frequent words is set to 10^{-5} in the model with 15 iterations. We also use full softmax to obtain the probability distribution.

We use AIDA (Elfardy and Diab, 2013) as the dialect identification tool. AIDA also provides a list of MSA equivalents for identified DA words in context.

[1] 41 LDC catalogs including data prepared for GALE and BOLT projects.

	BLEU	METEOR	TER	WER	PER
BASELINE1	20.6	27.5	65.9	69.2	45.3
BASELINE2	20.1	27.2	68.3	71.6	46.6
BASELINE3	21.3	28.0	65.2	68.6	44.6
PARL	20.7	27.1	67.5	69.6	45.5
WC_{cor}	20.9	27.7	65.4	68.7	44.8
PARL+WC	21.0	27.7	66.2	68.5	45.3
PARL+WC_{cor}	21.3	27.9	65.5	**68.0**	**44.5**

Table 1: Evaluation results (BLEU, METEOR (Banerjee and Lavie, 2005), TER (Snover et al., 2006), WER, PER) on the Bolt-arz test set compared to the baselines.

SMT System We use Moses decoder (Koehn et al., 2007) to build a standard phrase-based SMT system. Feature weights are tuned to maximize BLEU score on the tuning set using Minimum Error Rate Training (MERT) (Och, 2003) algorithm. Final results are reported by averaging over three tuning sessions with random initialization. Significant test is also performed to make sure that gains in the results are statistically significant. We use the implementation of Clark et al. (2011) to compute the p-value via approximate randomization algorithms. Since AIDA generates MSA equivalents in the lemma form, we use a factored translation model with lemma and POS factors. We use GIZA++ (Och and Ney, 2003) to word align the parallel corpus. We use SRILM (Stolcke and others, 2002) to build 5-gram language models with modified Kneser-Ney smoothing (Kneser and Ney, 1995). Our language modeling data consists of three data sets: a) The English Gigaword 5 (Graff and Cieri, 2003); b) The English side of the BOLT Phase 1 parallel data; and, c) different LDC English corpora collected from discussion forums.[2].

The translation model is trained using the MSA part of $\mathcal{D}_{ME}$ with 29M words. Therefore, any improvement in translating DA words on the test set is gained by our false friend identification and disambiguation approach. Our test set comprises 16K tokenized EGY words and is acquired by selecting 1065 sentences from LDC2012E30 (BOLT-arz-test). The tuning set contains 1547 sentences obtained from multiple LDC catalogs[3] and comprises 20k tokens.

[2]LDC2012E04, LDC2012E16, LDC2012E21, LDC2012E54

[3]LDC2012E15, LDC2012E19, LDC2012E55

5 Results and Discussion

The main goal of this work is to improve the translation chosen by SMT for a false friend based on its surrounding context. The final SMT performance is affected by two factors: First, the accuracy of false friend identifier and disambiguator. Second, the quality of predefined candidates generated by AIDA (FF are then replaced by one of these candidates chosen by WC).

In order to accurately evaluate the quality of our identification and disambiguation process, we design three different baselines. As the first baseline, we randomly tag EGY words which have been observed as MSA in the train data as false friend. False friends then are replaced by a randomly selected sense from respective candidates list (BASELINE1). As the second baseline, we follow the setup introduced in (Aminian et al., 2014). In this baseline, all EGY words that meet mentioned criteria, are replaced with one randomly selected sense from the list of candidates (BASELINE2). As the third baseline, we use the results of the raw baseline without any replacement (BASELINE3). The first two baselines can be used to evaluate the accuracy of FF identifier and disambiguator modules. The last baseline evaluates the overall effectiveness of the approach to enhance EGY-EN SMT which depends on both factors mentioned before.

The first three rows of Table 1 show BASELINE1, BASELINE2 and BASELINE3 results on our test set. PARL in the fourth row demonstrates the setup that only parallel data is exploited to identify false friends. The identified DA word is then replaced by a randomly selected MSA sense from the candidate

Ref.	i will tell you a story , and you judge whose fault it is .
Baseline	**Tb** AnA H+ AHky l+ HDrp +k mwqf w+ tqwly myn Ally glTAn
Replacement	**tmAm** AnA H+ AHky l+ HDrp +k mwqf w+ tqwly myn Ally glTAn
Baseline Trans.	ok , i am going to talk to you and say who was wrong .
Replacement Trans.	i will talk to you stand and say who was wrong .

Table 2: Example of correct FF identification and replacement with non-improving BLEU score.

list. Similarly, WC_{cor} shows the setup where WC is directly used to identify and replace false friends. In this setup, original EGY word is manually added to the list of MSA candidates generated by AIDA. Thus, WC module selects the most adequate candidate based on the context from the list containing both MSA equivalents and original EGY word. In other words, WC simultaneously performs FF identification and sense disambiguation. PARL+WC refers to the system that uses PARL to identify FF and then WC to disambiguate them. It is to be emphasized that in this setup, WC chooses the most appropriate MSA equivalent of each false friend only from the list of candidates generated by AIDA. We also define PARL+WC_{cor} in which WC_{cor} is used as a FF identifier as well as disambiguator (similar to the second setup above). In fact, we prevent mistakes from PARL by using WC as an identifier as well. This setup replaces a word by its MSA equivalent only if both PARL and WC identify it as FF.

As shown in Table 1, all replacement experiments outperform BASELINE1 and BASELINE2 in terms of BLEU score. PARL improves BASELINE1 and BASELINE2 BLEU scores by 0.1% absolute (0.5% relative) and 0.6% absolute (3% relative) receptively. This implies that our FF identifier achieves more accurate FF predictions compared to random and blind predictions.

Using WC_{cor} for FF identification and disambiguation shows a noticeable improvement over the case that we just use PARL for identification (in terms of BLEU, WER and PER). This shows that contextual similarity plays a more important role compared to the information extracted from parallel data to train a FF identification model. PARL is also too sensitive to errors in the word alignment. So noise in the alignment will lead to incorrect prediction and thereby, inadequate replacement.

As expected, combining PARL and WC for FF identification and replacement (PARL+WC) outperforms the individual decisions made by each module solely. This setup benefits from evidences provided by both modules for FF identification and sense disambiguation. Eventually, the last setup PARL+WC_{cor} leads to 0.3% absolute (1.4% relative) BLEU improvement over PARL+WC. It also outperforms PARL+WC in terms of other SMT evaluation metrics such as METEOR, TER, WER and PER. For example, it achieves 0.7%, 0.5% and 0.8% reduction in TER, WER and PER respectively compared to PARL+WC. In the last setup, we just replace words which both PARL and WC commonly identify them as FF. In other words, WC refines some of the PARL mistakes and avoids it from replacing words which are mistakenly identified as FF by PARL . It is worth noting that significant tests show that all gains in the BLEU, METEOR and TER over BASELINE2 and BASELINE3 are statistically significant at the 95% level.

Our best performing setup, PARL+WC_{cor}, reduces BASELINE3 WER and PER by the noticeable amount of 0.6% and 0.1% respectively. This indicates that our approach has the power to enhance SMT lexical choice and select more accurate target translations for the false friends. However, our method does not outperform BASELINE3 BLEU score. Our analysis shows that the main reason for this phenomenon is that the SMT translation table does not contain adequate bilingual phrase pairs for some of the replaced MSA equivalents (suggested by AIDA). Thus, decoder can not generate coherent phrases while translating these words. As an example, consider the sentence shown in Table 2. Word '*Tb*' in the baseline sentence means *all right*, *very well* or *ok* in EGY while it means *medicine* when used as MSA. Our FF identifier has correctly identified this word as a FF. The disambiguator module also has adequately replaced word 'Tb' with the MSA word 'tmAm' which means *ok*. However, this replacement does not yield to a better translation for this word. This happens because word 'tmAm' has not been observed as an interjection in our SMT phrase table. Thus, SMT decoder is not able to find a good translation for this word.

	BASELINE1	BASELINE2	BASELINE3
PARL	37.7/38.5	41.5/40.3	34.7/44.2
PARL+WC	38.7/32.8	45.5/36.4	34.0/35.2
PARL+WC_{cor}	40.5/32.2	46.4/36.3	35.7/35.1

Table 3: Percentage of BLEU-enhanced sentences/percentage of BLEU-degraded sentences for different replacement approaches compared to each baseline separately.

We conducted another analysis to closely assess the impact of our disambiguator module (WC) in improving target sentences BLEU score. We ran our replacement setups on the proportion of Boltarz sentences which contain at least one FF. FF are predicted by PARL module. We ended up getting a set with 796 sentences. Table 3 shows the percentage of BLEU-enhanced and BLEU-degraded sentences in this set for each setup compared to the baselines separately. The setup which exploits WC_{cor} for FF identification and disambiguation is excluded from this comparison as it does not use PARL for FF identification. As the percentages in Table 3 indicate, PARL+WC noticeably increases (decreases) percentage of BLEU-enhanced (BLEU-degraded) sentences compared to PARL setup with respect to BASELINE1 and BASELINE2. As shown before (Table 1), the last setup PARL+WC_{cor} did not improve BASELINE3 BLEU score. However, results in Table 3 show that this setup increases percentage of BLEU-enhanced sentences compared to PARL+WC and PARL with respect to BASELINE3 significantly. Comparing percentages of BLEU-degraded sentences for mentioned setups gives the same results.

Table 4 shows some translation examples with and without any replacement. The replacement is done using our best-performing setup PARL+WC_{cor} on Bolt-arz test set. The first four examples demonstrate cases that FF (shown in bold) are correctly identified and replaced with a proper MSA equivalent. For instance, the word 'zy' in the first example means *uniform* or *clothing* in MSA and *such as* or *like* in EGY. Thus, replacing the word 'zy' with MSA word 'mvl' which means *like* yields to better translation and thereby, improves BLEU score.

In the second example, word 'nsyb' which means *forget* in this context is replaced with MSA equivalent 'trk' that means *leave* or *forget*. As the result, decoder has translated phrase 'trk +nA mn AlAxtlAf' into a longer phrase *let us from the difference* instead of generating an incoherent translation such as baseline.

Word 'wHcp' in the third example is not a pure EGY word. However, it conveys a meaning different from its observed senses in the phrase table. Hence, baseline incorrectly translates this word to *difficult* while the replaced setup generate the correct translation *bad* for the replaced MSA equivalent 'syC'. Hence, as shown, our approach has improved SMT lexical choice significantly in this example.

Word 'cwf' in the fourth example is also correctly identified as a FF according to context. This word is used as noun in MSA with meanings *look* and *appearance* while it is used as a command verb (*order someone to look*) in EGY. As we can see, our disambiguator module has adequately replaced this word with the verb 'rAy' which means *to look at* or *to see*. As the result, the decoder has translated this word into the word *see* in the English sentence which leads to higher BLEU score compared to the baseline translation.

Word 'Erkp' in the fifth example has English equivalent *battle* in EGY and *test* in MSA context. Similar to the previous example, baseline selects the incorrect translation *testing*. While our replacement setup substitues this word with MSA equivalent 'mErkp' which means *battle* and thereby, improves the translation.

Sixth instance in Table 2 demonstrates the example where our FF identifier has incorrectly identified word 'HAjp' (*need* in this context) as FF. This word is then replaced by the word 'Amr' (*order*) which does not convey the original word meaning according to context. Hence, the decoder is not able to find a proper translation for the replaced word in the context.

Ref.	not private , i mean like buses and the metro and trains ... etc .
Baseline	mc mlkyp xASp yEny AqSd **zy** AlAtwbys w+ Almtrw w+ AlqTAr . . . Alx
Replacement	mc mlkyp xASp yEny AqSd **mvl** AlAtwbys w+ Almtrw w+ AlqTAr . . . Alx
Baseline Trans.	privately , i mean , i mean , i do not like the bus and subway train , etc .
Replacement Trans.	not privately , i mean , i mean , such as the bus and subway train , etc .
Ref.	let us forget about our differences and unite .
Baseline	**nsyb** +nA mn AlAxtlAf w+ ntwHd
Replacement	**trk** +nA mn AlAxtlAf w+ ntwHd
Baseline Trans.	we disagree and suffering from
Replacement Trans.	let us from the difference and unify
Ref.	and those who said that the girls ... indeed , i heard very bad words , why ?
Baseline	w+ Ally yqwl AlbnAt . . . b+ jd smEt AllfAZ **wHcp** qwy lyh kdh
Replacement	w+ Ally yqwl AlbnAt . . . b+ jd smEt AllfAZ **syC** qwy lyh kdh
Baseline Trans.	and to say ... very very difficult . that is why i heard
Replacement Trans.	and to say ... seriously , i heard a strong bad , why ?
Ref.	at least three parties ; check them and read about them in detail
Baseline	Ely AlAql three AHzAb **cwf** +hm w+ AqrA +hm b+ Emq
Replacement	Ely AlAql three AHzAb **rAy** +hm w+ AqrA +hm b+ Emq
Baseline Trans.	at least three of the depth of them and with them .
Replacement Trans.	at least three parties see them and baqir them in depth
Ref.	it is waiting for disagreement between the salafis and the liberals , which engages them in a new battle of nonsense speech similar to
Baseline	yntZr An yxtlf Alslfywn mE AllybrAlyyn f+ ydxlwA fy **Erkp** Ely +k jdydp mn qbyl rmy
Replacement	yntZr An yxtlf Alslfywn mE AllybrAlyyn f+ ydxlwA fy **mErkp** Ely +k jdydp mn qbyl rmy
Baseline Trans.	it is expected that the salafis disagrees with liberals , in testing on your new prior to throw
Replacement Trans.	waiting for the salafis disagrees with liberals , in the battle for your new prior to throw
Ref.	also eradication of poverty and need is very important , toqua
Baseline	w+ kmAn AlqDAC Ely Alfqr w+ **HAjp** mhm jdA yA+ tqy
Replacement	w+ kmAn AlqDAC Ely Alfqr w+ **Amr** kbyr jdA yA+ tqy
Baseline Trans.	and also the eradication of poverty and need is very important ,
Replacement Trans.	and also the eradication of poverty and a very large ,

Table 4: Translation examples with and without replacement drawn from Bolt-arz test

6 Conclusion and Future Work

We presented a new approach for improving cross-language SMT performance without any in-domain training data by identifying false friends and replacing them with a semantically similar equivalent from the standard language. We show that our approach improves lexical choice in EGY-EN SMT system trained only on MSA data. We demonstrate a fully unsupervised approach for false friend identification and disambiguation using evidences extracted from parallel and monolingual data. We showed that our best-performing setup reduces the baseline WER and PER by the noticeable amount of 0.6% and 0.1% respectively. One interesting line to expand this study is exploring an automatic way to generate the list of possible equivalents for FF instead of using a predefined inventory of senses. One idea is benefiting from continues word vectors and their similarity to extract possible word senses for a particular FF from available monolingual corpus.

Acknowledgments

This work was supported by the Defense Advanced Research Projects Agency (DARPA) Contract No. HR0011-12-C-0014, the BOLT program with subcontract from Raytheon BBN. We would like to acknowledge the useful comments by three anonymous reviewers who helped in making this publication more concise and better presented.

References

Maryam Aminian, Mahmoud Ghoneim, and Mona Diab. 2014. Handling oov words in dialectal arabic to english machine translation. In *Proceedings of the EMNLP'2014 Workshop on Language Technology for Closely Related Languages and Language Variants*, pages 99–108, Doha, Qatar, October. Association for Computational Linguistics.

Satanjeev Banerjee and Alon Lavie. 2005. METEOR: An automatic metric for MT evaluation with improved correlation with human judgments. In *Proceedings of the ACL Workshop on Intrinsic and Extrinsic Evaluation Measures for Machine Translation and/or Summarization*, pages 65–72, Ann Arbor, Michigan, June. Association for Computational Linguistics.

Keith Brown and Keith Allan. 2010. *Concise encyclopedia of semantics*. Elsevier.

Marine Carpuat and Dekai Wu. 2005. Word sense disambiguation vs. statistical machine translation. In *Proceedings of the 43rd Annual Meeting of the Association for Computational Linguistics (ACL'05)*, pages 387–394, Ann Arbor, Michigan, June. Association for Computational Linguistics.

Marine Carpuat and Dekai Wu. 2007. Improving statistical machine translation using word sense disambiguation. In *Proceedings of the 2007 Joint Conference on Empirical Methods in Natural Language Processing and Computational Natural Language Learning (EMNLP-CoNLL)*, pages 61–72, Prague, Czech Republic, June. Association for Computational Linguistics.

Yee Seng Chan, Hwee Tou Ng, and David Chiang. 2007. Word sense disambiguation improves statistical machine translation. In *Proceedings of the 45th Annual Meeting of the Association of Computational Linguistics*, pages 33–40, Prague, Czech Republic, June. Association for Computational Linguistics.

Jonathan H. Clark, Chris Dyer, Alon Lavie, and Noah A. Smith. 2011. Better hypothesis testing for statistical machine translation: Controlling for optimizer instability. In *Proceedings of the 49th Annual Meeting of the Association for Computational Linguistics: Human Language Technologies*, pages 176–181, Portland, Oregon, USA, June. Association for Computational Linguistics.

Heba Elfardy and Mona Diab. 2013. Sentence level dialect identification in arabic. In *Proceedings of the 51st Annual Meeting of the Association for Computational Linguistics (Volume 2: Short Papers)*, pages 456–461, Sofia, Bulgaria, August. Association for Computational Linguistics.

Yoav Freund and Robert E Schapire. 1999. Large margin classification using the perceptron algorithm. *Machine learning*, 37(3):277–296.

Oana Frunza and Diana Inkpen. 2006. Semi-supervised learning of partial cognates using bilingual bootstrapping. In *Proceedings of the 21st International Conference on Computational Linguistics and 44th Annual Meeting of the Association for Computational Linguistics*, pages 441–448, Sydney, Australia, July. Association for Computational Linguistics.

David Graff and Christopher Cieri. 2003. English gigaword, ldc catalog no.: Ldc2003t05. *LDC2003T05. Linguistic Data Consortium, University of Pennsylvania*.

Nizar Y Habash. 2010. Introduction to arabic natural language processing. *Synthesis Lectures on Human Language Technologies*, 3(1):1–187.

Diana Inkpen, Oana Frunza, and Grzegorz Kondrak. 2005. Automatic identification of cognates and false friends in french and english. In *Proceedings of the International Conference Recent Advances in Natural Language Processing*, pages 251–257.

Reinhard Kneser and Hermann Ney. 1995. Improved backing-off for m-gram language modeling. In *Acoustics, Speech, and Signal Processing, 1995. ICASSP-95., 1995 International Conference on*, volume 1, pages 181–184. IEEE.

Philipp Koehn, Hieu Hoang, Alexandra Birch, Chris Callison-Burch, Marcello Federico, Nicola Bertoldi, Brooke Cowan, Wade Shen, Christine Moran, Richard Zens, Chris Dyer, Ondrej Bojar, Alexandra Constantin, and Evan Herbst. 2007. Moses: Open source toolkit for statistical machine translation. In *Proceedings of the 45th Annual Meeting of the Association for Computational Linguistics Companion Volume Proceedings of the Demo and Poster Sessions*, pages 177–180, Prague, Czech Republic, June. Association for Computational Linguistics.

Grzegorz Kondrak. 2001. Identifying cognates by phonetic and semantic similarity. In *Proceedings of the second meeting of the North American Chapter of the Association for Computational Linguistics on Language technologies*, pages 1–8. Association for Computational Linguistics.

Mohamed Maamouri, Ann Bies, Tim Buckwalter, and Wigdan Mekki. 2004. The penn arabic treebank: Building a large-scale annotated arabic corpus. In *NEMLAR conference on Arabic language resources and tools*, pages 102–109.

Tomas Mikolov, Ilya Sutskever, Kai Chen, Greg S Corrado, and Jeff Dean. 2013. Distributed representations of words and phrases and their compositionality. In *Advances in Neural Information Processing Systems*, pages 3111–3119.

George A Miller. 1995. Wordnet: a lexical database for english. *Communications of the ACM*, 38(11):39–41.

Ruslan Mitkov, Viktor Pekar, Dimitar Blagoev, and Andrea Mulloni. 2007. Methods for extracting and classifying pairs of cognates and false friends. *Machine translation*, 21(1):29–53.

Andrea Mulloni, V Pekar, R Mitkov, and D Blagoev. 2007. Semantic evidence for automatic identification of cognates. In *Proceedings of the RANLP2007 workshop: Acquisition and management of multilingual lexicons*, pages 49–54. Citeseer.

Svetlin Nakov, Preslav Nakov, and Elena Paskaleva. 2007. Cognate or false friend? ask the web. In *Proceedings of the RANLP2007 workshop: Acquisition and management of multilingual lexicons*, pages 55–62.

Svetlin Nakov, Preslav Nakov, and Elena Paskaleva. 2009. Unsupervised extraction of false friends from parallel bi-texts using the web as a corpus. In *Proceedings of the International Conference RANLP-2009*, pages 292–298, Borovets, Bulgaria, September. Association for Computational Linguistics.

Franz Josef Och and Hermann Ney. 2003. A systematic comparison of various statistical alignment models. *Computational linguistics*, 29(1):19–51.

Franz Josef Och. 2003. Minimum error rate training in statistical machine translation. In *Proceedings of the 41st Annual Meeting of the Association for Computational Linguistics*, pages 160–167, Sapporo, Japan, July. Association for Computational Linguistics.

Kishore Papineni, Salim Roukos, Todd Ward, and Wei-Jing Zhu. 2002. Bleu: a method for automatic evaluation of machine translation. In *Proceedings of 40th Annual Meeting of the Association for Computational Linguistics*, pages 311–318, Philadelphia, Pennsylvania, USA, July. Association for Computational Linguistics.

Arfath Pasha, Mohamed Al-Badrashiny, Mona Diab, Ahmed El Kholy, Ramy Eskander, Nizar Habash, Manoj Pooleery, Owen Rambow, and Ryan Roth. 2014. Madamira: A fast, comprehensive tool for morphological analysis and disambiguation of arabic. In Nicoletta Calzolari, Khalid Choukri, Thierry Declerck, Hrafn Loftsson, Bente Maegaard, Joseph Mariani, Asuncion Moreno, Jan Odijk, and Stelios Piperidis, editors, *Proceedings of the Ninth International Conference on Language Resources and Evaluation (LREC'14)*, pages 1094–1101, Reykjavik, Iceland, May. European Language Resources Association (ELRA). ACL Anthology Identifier: L14-1479.

Helmut Schmid. 1994. Probabilistic part-of-speech tagging using decision trees. In *Proceedings of the international conference on new methods in language processing*, volume 12, pages 44–49. Citeseer.

Stefan Schulz, Kornel Markó, Eduardo Sbrissia, Percy Nohama, and Udo Hahn. 2004. Cognate mapping - a heuristic strategy for the semi-supervised acquisition of a spanish lexicon from a portuguese seed lexicon. In *Proceedings of Coling 2004*, pages 813–819, Geneva, Switzerland, Aug 23–Aug 27. COLING.

Matthew Snover, Bonnie Dorr, Richard Schwartz, Linnea Micciulla, and John Makhoul. 2006. A study of translation edit rate with targeted human annotation. In *Proceedings of association for machine translation in the Americas*, pages 223–231.

Andreas Stolcke et al. 2002. Srilm an extensible language modeling toolkit. In *INTERSPEECH*.

Christoph Tillmann, Stephan Vogel, Hermann Ney, Arkaitz Zubiaga, and Hassan Sawaf. 1997. Accelerated dp based search for statistical translation. In *Proceedings of Eurospeech'97*, pages 2667–2670.

David Vickrey, Luke Biewald, Marc Teyssier, and Daphne Koller. 2005. Word-sense disambiguation for machine translation. In *Proceedings of Human Language Technology Conference and Conference on Empirical Methods in Natural Language Processing*, pages 771–778, Vancouver, British Columbia, Canada, October. Association for Computational Linguistics.

Zhibiao Wu and Martha Palmer. 1994. Verb semantics and lexical selection. In *Proceedings of the 32nd Annual Meeting of the Association for Computational Linguistics*, pages 133–138, Las Cruces, New Mexico, USA, June. Association for Computational Linguistics.

Mei Yang and Katrin Kirchhoff. 2012. Unsupervised translation disambiguation for cross-domain statistical machine translation. In *Proceedings of association for machine translation in the Americas*.

METEOR-WSD: Improved Sense Matching in MT Evaluation

Marianna Apidianaki
LIMSI-CNRS, Orsay, France
marianna@limsi.fr

Benjamin Marie
LIMSI-CNRS, Orsay, France
Lingua et Machina, Le Chesnay, France
benjamin.marie@limsi.fr

Abstract

We present an initial experiment in integrating a disambiguation step in MT evaluation. We show that accounting for sense distinctions helps METEOR establish better sense correspondences and improves its correlation with human judgments of translation quality.

1 Introduction

Synonym and paraphrase support are useful means for capturing lexical variation in Machine Translation evaluation. In the METEOR metric (Banerjee and Lavie, 2005), some level of abstraction from the surface forms of words is achieved through the "stem" and "synonymy" modules which map words with the same stem or belonging to the same WordNet synset (Fellbaum, 1998). METEOR-NEXT (Denkowski and Lavie, 2010) extends semantic mapping to languages other than English and to longer text segments, using the paraphrase tables constructed by the *pivot* method (Bannard and Callison-Burch, 2005). Although both metrics yield improvements regarding correlation with human judgments of translation quality compared to the standard METEOR configuration for English, they integrate semantic information in a rather simplistic way: matching is performed without disambiguation, which means that all the variants available for a particular text fragment are treated as semantically equivalent. This is however not always the case, as synonyms found in different WordNet synsets correspond to different senses. Similarly, paraphrase sets obtained by the pivot method often group phrases describing different senses (Apidianaki et al., 2014). In these cases, a word sense disambiguation (WSD) step would help to identify the correct synset or subset of paraphrases for a word or phrase in context and avoid erroneous matchings between text segments carrying different senses. We present an initial experiment on the integration of a disambiguation step in the METEOR metric and show how it helps increase correlation with human judgments of translation quality.

2 Disambiguation in METEOR

We apply the metric to translations of news texts from the five languages involved in the WMT14 Metrics Shared Task (Machacek and Bojar, 2014) (French, Hindi, German, Czech, Russian) into English. We disambiguate the English references – different for each language pair – using the Babelfy tool (Moro et al., 2014), which performs graph-based WSD by exploiting the structure of the multilingual network BabelNet (Navigli and Ponzetto, 2012). The assigned annotations are multilingual synsets grouping word and phrase variants in different languages coming from various sources (WordNet, Wikipedia, etc.) and carrying the same sense. We use the WordNet literals found in the sense selected by Babelfy to filter the WordNet synonym sets used in METEOR and prevent METEOR from considering erroneous matchings as correct.[1] As a result, only the synonyms found in the proposed BabelNet synset are kept and considered as correct by METEOR, while synonyms corresponding to other

[1]In future work, we intend to apply the same filtering to paraphrases in different languages.

Proceedings of SSST-9, Ninth Workshop on Syntax, Semantics and Structure in Statistical Translation, pages 49–51,
Denver, Colorado, June 4, 2015.

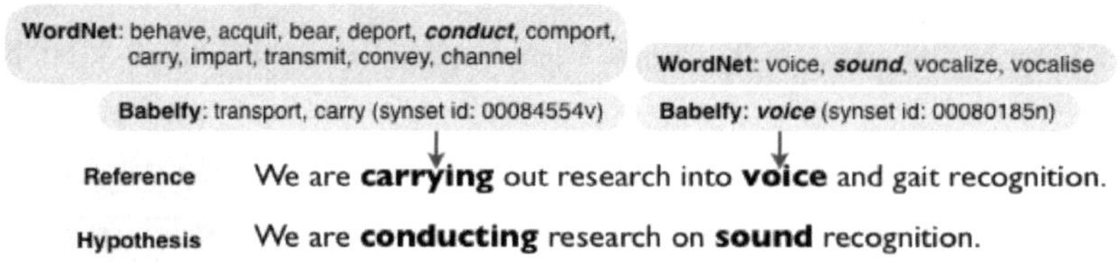

Figure 1: Good and erroneous matchings made by the synonymy module and WSD.

senses are discarded. METEOR is a tunable metric able to assign a weight to each of its modules in order to better correlate with human judgments. Since METEOR needs to perform a costly grid-search on 8 parameters, we did not re-optimize the weights due to time constraints. Considering this, the following experiments are made in a suboptimal configuration as we can expect a re-optimization to take the impact of the disambiguation into account more efficiently.

3 Results

In Table 1, we present the results obtained for four different configurations: METEOR with WordNet synonym support vs METEOR with WSD, with and without paraphrasing. The scores correspond to segment-level Kentall τ correlations of the metric with human judgments of translation quality. When the paraphrase module is activated, WSD slightly improves the correlation of the metric to human judgments in all languages except for Czech. Nevertheless, it is worth noting that this would improve METEOR's ranking in the results of the WMT14 shared task for French-English, which would then be ranked 4th, instead of 7th, among 18 participants.

When the WSD prediction is correct, it permits to avoid erroneous matchings between synonyms corresponding to different WordNet senses. In the example given in Figure 1, the synonymy module creates a wrong mapping between *sound* and *voice*. As *sound* is not contained in the BabelNet synset selected by the WSD component, this avoids establishing an erroneous match. Given, however, that WSD does not always succeed, the paraphrase module manages to find correspondences in cases of wrong disambiguation choices. This is the case illustrated by the first annotation in Figure 1 where the synset proposed by the WSD tool describes the "transport" sense. This wrong WSD prediction establishes no match but the paraphrase module that operates after WSD, manages to map *carrying* and *conducting*. When the paraphrase module is deactivated, the correlation of METEOR-WSD is lower than that of the basic METEOR configuration. Although the disambiguation discards erroneous matchings made by the synonymy module, there is no means to correct erroneous disambiguation choices without the paraphrases.

METEOR configuration		fr-en	de-en	hi-en	cs-en	ru-en
w/ par.	METEOR	.406	.334	.420	**.282**	.329
	METEOR-WSD	**.410**	**.335**	**.422**	.278	**.331**
w/o par.	METEOR	.400	.326	.401	.271	.313
	METEOR-WSD	.403	.321	.396	.263	.312

Table 1: Segment-level Kendall's τ correlations between METEOR and the official human judgments of the WMT14 metrics shared task.

4 Conclusion and Perspectives

Our results demonstrate the beneficial impact of disambiguation in MT evaluation. Accounting for sense distinctions helps METEOR establish better quality correspondences between hypotheses and human references. In future work, we intend to experiment with other WSD methods such as the alignment-based method recently proposed by Apidianaki and Gong (2015). Moreover, we plan to integrate a WSD step in evaluation for languages other than English. We expect to observe substantial improvements in languages where the synonymy module is unavailable and where the quality of pivot paraphrases is lower than in English. We also plan to conduct experiments using METEOR-WSD for tuning a Statistical Machine Translation system and expect to observe improvements in translation quality compared to the same system tuned with METEOR without WSD.

References

Marianna Apidianaki and Li Gong. 2015. LIMSI: Translations as Source of Indirect Supervision for Multilingual All-Words Sense Disambiguation and Entity Linking. In *Proceedings of the 9th International Workshop on Semantic Evaluation (SemEval-2015)*, Denver, Colorado, USA.

Marianna Apidianaki, Emilia Verzeni, and Diana Mccarthy. 2014. Semantic Clustering of Pivot Paraphrases. In *Proceedings of the Ninth International Conference on Language Resources and Evaluation (LREC'14)*, Reykjavik, Iceland.

Satanjeev Banerjee and Alon Lavie. 2005. METEOR: An Automatic Metric for MT Evaluation with Improved Correlation with Human Judgments. In *Proceedings of the ACL Workshop on Intrinsic and Extrinsic Evaluation Measures for Machine Translation and/or Summarization*, pages 65–72, Ann Arbor, Michigan, USA.

Colin Bannard and Chris Callison-Burch. 2005. Paraphrasing with Bilingual Parallel Corpora. In *Proceedings of the 43rd Annual Meeting of the Association for Computational Linguistics (ACL'05)*, pages 597–604, Ann Arbor, Michigan, USA.

Michael Denkowski and Alon Lavie. 2010. Extending the METEOR Machine Translation Evaluation Metric to the Phrase Level. In *Human Language Technologies: The 2010 Annual Conference of the North American Chapter of the Association for Computational Linguistics*, pages 250–253, Los Angeles, California, USA.

Christiane Fellbaum, editor. 1998. *WordNet: an electronic lexical database*. MIT Press.

Matous Machacek and Ondrej Bojar. 2014. Results of the WMT14 Metrics Shared Task. In *Proceedings of the Ninth Workshop on Statistical Machine Translation*, pages 293–301, Baltimore, Maryland, USA.

Andrea Moro, Alessandro Raganato, and Roberto Navigli. 2014. Entity Linking meets Word Sense Disambiguation: a Unified Approach. *Transactions of the Association for Computational Linguistics (TACL)*, 2:231–244.

Roberto Navigli and Simone Paolo Ponzetto. 2012. BabelNet: The Automatic Construction, Evaluation and Application of a Wide-Coverage Multilingual Semantic Network. *Artificial Intelligence*, 193:217–250.

Analyzing English-Spanish Named-Entity enhanced Machine Translation

Mikel Artetxe, Eneko Agirre, Inaki Alegria, Gorka Labaka
IXA NLP Group, University of the Basque Country (UPV/EHU)
{martetxe003@ikasle., e.agirre@, i.alegria@, gorka.labaka@}ehu.eus

Abstract

Translation of named-entities (NEs) is an issue in SMT. In this paper we analyze the errors when translating NEs with a SMT system from English to Spanish. We train on Europarl and test on News Commentary, focusing on entities correctly recognized by an automatic NE recognition system. The automatic systems translate around 85% NEs correctly, leaving a small margin for improving performance. In addition, we implement a purpose-build NE translator and integrate it in the SMT system, yielding a small but significant improvement in BLEU score. Our analysis shows that, contrary to similar systems translating from Chinese to English, there was no improvement in NE translation, prompting further work.

1 Introduction

Name-Aware SMT focuses on improving named-entity (NE) translation. The most basic approach is to add a devoted named-entity translation lexicon to the training data. Pal et al. (2010) report good results using this method. Another common solution is to replace NEs with special tags and translate them in a postedition step. For instance, Okuma et al. (2008) propose substituting source names with high frequency names before applying SMT. In a more sophisticated setting, Li et al. (2013) use hierarchical SMT (HSMT) to integrate a specialized NE translation system, showing relevant improvements in overall translation quality and, particularly, in NE translation when translating from Chinese to English. In this paper we replicate their system and analyze how NEs are translated when translating from English to Spanish. There is also related work on including transliteration modules (Hermjakob et al., 2008).

2 Analysis of NE translation in SMT

In order to better understand how traditional SMT systems perform when translating NE from English to Spanish, we carried out a manual analysis over 525 sentences that were randomly taken from the news-test2011 test set as given in the shared task of the NAACL 2012 workshop on SMT, which we used as our development set. We noted that, in some cases, both Spanish and English text seemed to be actual translations from a third language.

We first run the ixa-pipe-nerc Named-Entity Recognition and Classification (NERC) system (Agerri et al., 2014) in these sentences, and manually assessed the correctness of each of the 536 NEs that it recognized, as shown in Table 1. We then identified how each of the correctly recognized NEs was translated in the reference translations. We discovered that 1.61% of them were missing in the translations, 3.63% were not translated correctly, and another 2.82% had a meaningful but indirect translation (e.g. a country name translated as a demonym). This means that, even in the human translation, only 91.94% of the NEs had a correct NE translation in the reference translation.

We then checked the performance of a HSMT system trained on Europarl v7 using Moses (Koehn et al., 2007). Table 2 shows the amount of correctly translated NEs for this system, according to their class and number of occurrences in the training corpus. The results suggest that our baseline system performs relatively well for this task (86% overall), and that the errors are concentrated on NEs with zero or one occurrences (approx. 77% accuracy), with very good performance for NEs occurring more than

Proceedings of SSST-9, Ninth Workshop on Syntax, Semantics and Structure in Statistical Translation, pages 52–54,
Denver, Colorado, June 4, 2015.

Correct				Wrong
Person	Location	Organization	Misc.	
123 (22.95%)	184 (34.33%)	132 (24.63%)	57 (10.63%)	40 (7.46%)

Table 1: Distribution of NEs in the development set

	Person	Location	Organization	Misc.	Total
0 occurrence	92/104 (88.46%)	40/51 (78.43%)	45/71 (63.38%)	5/10 (50%)	182/236 (77.12%)
1 occurrence	2/2 (100%)	6/7 (85.71%)	5/8 (62.5%)	1/1 (100%)	14/18 (77.78%)
>1 occurrences	17/17 (100%)	125/126 (99.21%)	49/53 (92.45%)	38/46 (82.61%)	229/242 (94.63%)
Total	111/123 (90.24%)	171/184 (92.93%)	99/132 (75%)	44/57 (77.19%)	425/496 (85.69%)

Table 2: NE translation accuracy in the development set for the baseline HSMT system.

	Baseline HSMT	NE enhanced HSMT
BLEU score	31.01	31.21
NE translation accuracy	414 (87.34%)	415 (87.55%)

Table 3: NE translation accuracy and BLEU score in the test set

once. We analyzed the errors and found that 28.17% of them corresponded to untranslated NEs, whereas another 23.94% were caused by proper nouns that were translated as common nouns even though they should have been kept unchanged.

In conclusion, we can say that, compared to Chinese-English (Li et al., 2013), the room of improvement is very small (roughly 15% vs. 30%), and focused on OOV and hapax legomena NEs.

3 NE-enhanced HSMT system

Our approach for improving NE translation in SMT is based on the framework proposed by Li et al. (2013). We train a HSMT system with Moses, adapting the training phase to treat each NE class as a non-terminal. Given our analysis (cf. Section 2), NE occurring more than once are left for the HSMT to handle. In the case of NEs with zero or one occurrences, we use a specialized module to generate additional translations that are added to the phrase table on the fly. This module merges the results of several independent techniques to translate NEs: an automatically extracted dictionary, a human dictionary, Wikipedia, leaving the NE unchanged, a special treatment for title + person structures, a RBMT engine and an SMT system specialized on NE. Each translation technique is given an independent weight, and the system is tuned to optimize these weights.

We used news-test2012 as our test set and took 525 random sentences to measure NE translation accuracy and the full test set to calculate the BLEU score. Table 3 shows the results obtained by this system in comparison with the baseline system (cf. Section 2). Our results show a small but statistically significant improvement of 0.2 BLEU points, but no improvement in terms of NE translation accuracy. Note that 7.17% of the NEs were translated differently. We are currently studying the reasons of the improvement in BLEU.

4 Conclusions and future work

In this paper we have analyzed the performance of an English to Spanish HSMT system, concluding that there is a small margin for improvement for NE translation. We detected that a non-negligible percentage is not translated as a correct NE in the reference translation. In addition, we replicated a successful HSMT system incorporating a NE translation module (Li et al., 2013). Our NE-enhanced HSMT system achieves a significantly better BLEU score, but manual analysis shows that the performance is the same in terms of NE-translation accuracy. The presentation will include more details and examples of our analysis.

Our results show that when train and test data come from similar domains, the translation of NEs from English to Spanish performs quite well. We would like to explore out-of-domain settings.

Acknowledgements

This work was partially funded by the European Commission (QTLEAP – FP7-ICT-2013.4.1-610516).

References

Rodrigo Agerri, Josu Bermudez, and German Rigau. 2014. Ixa pipeline: Efficient and Ready to Use Multilingual NLP tools. In *Proceedings of the 9th Language Resources and Evaluation Conference (LREC2014)*, pages 26–31.

Ulf Hermjakob, Kevin Knight, and Hal Daumé III. 2008. Name Translation in Statistical Machine Translation - Learning When to Transliterate. In *ACL*, pages 389–397.

Philipp Koehn, Hieu Hoang, Alexandra Birch, Chris Callison-Burch, Marcello Federico, Nicola Bertoldi, Brooke Cowan, Wade Shen, Christine Moran, Richard Zens, et al. 2007. Moses: Open Source Toolkit for Statistical Machine Translation. In *Proceedings of the 45th Annual Meeting of the ACL on Interactive Poster and Demonstration Sessions*, pages 177–180. Association for Computational Linguistics.

Haibo Li, Jing Zheng, Heng Ji, Qi Li, and Wen Wang. 2013. Name-aware Machine Translation. In *ACL 2013*, pages 604–614.

Hideo Okuma, Hirofumi Yamamoto, and Eiichiro Sumita. 2008. Introducing a translation dictionary into phrase-based SMT. *IEICE transactions on information and systems*, 91(7):2051–2057.

Santanu Pal, Sudip Kumar Naskar, Pavel Pecina, Sivaji Bandyopadhyay, and Andy Way. 2010. Handling Named Entities and Compound Verbs in Phrase-Based Statistical Machine Translation. In *Proceedings of the 2010 Workshop on Multiword Expressions: from Theory to Applications*. ACL.

Predicting Prepositions for SMT

Marion Weller[1,2], **Alexander Fraser**[2], **Sabine Schulte im Walde**[1]

[1] IMS, University of Stuttgart – (wellermn|schulte)@ims.uni-stuttgart.de
[2] CIS, Ludwig-Maximilian University of Munich – fraser@cis.uni-muenchen.de

Introduction The translation of prepositions is a difficult task for machine translation; a preposition must convey the source-side meaning and also meet target-side constraints. In our approach, we move the selection of prepositions out of the translation system into a post-processing component. During translation, we use an abstract representation of prepositions as a place-holder that serves as a basis for the generation of prepositions in the post-processing step: all subcategorized elements of a verb are considered and allotted to their respective functions – as PPs with an overt preposition or as NPs with an "empty" preposition, e.g. *to call for sth.* → $\emptyset$ *etw. erfordern*. The language model and the translation rules often fail to correctly model subcategorization in standard SMT systems because verbs and their subcategorized elements are often not adjacent.

We use a morphology-aware SMT system which first translates into a lemmatized representation with a component to generate fully inflected forms in a second step, see Toutanova et al. (2008) and Fraser et al. (2012). The inflection step requires the modeling of the grammatical *case* of noun phrases, which corresponds to determining the syntactic function. Weller et al. (2013) describe modeling *case* in SMT; we extend their setup to cover the prediction of prepositions in both PP and NPs (i.e., the "empty" preposition). The presented work is similar to that of Agirre et al. (2009), but is applied to a fully statistical MT system. A detailed presentation of our work including a full literature survey can be found in Weller et al. (2015).

Methodology To build the translation model, we use an abstract target-language representation in which nouns, adjectives and articles are lemmatized, and prepositions are substituted with place-holders. Additionally, "empty" place-holder prepositions are inserted at the beginning of noun phrases. To obtain a symmetric data structure, "empty" place-holders are also added to source-side NPs. When generating surface forms for the translation output, a phrase with a place-holder preposition can be realized as a noun phrase (empty preposition) or as a prepositional phrase by generating the preposition's surface form.

Figure 1 illustrates the process: for the English input with the extra null-prepositions (column 1), the SMT system outputs a lemmatized representation with place-holder prepositions (column 2). In a first step, prepositions and *case* for the SMT output are predicted (column 3). Then, the three remaining inflection-relevant morphological features *number*, *gender* and *strong/weak* are predicted on "regular" sentences without place-holders, given the prepositions from the previous step (column 4). In the last step, fully inflected forms are produced based on features and lemmas (column 5).

Abstract Representation and Prediction Features Initial experiments showed that replacing prepositions by simple place-holders decreases the translation quality. As an extension to the basic approach with plain place-holders, we thus experiment with enriching the place-holders such that they contain more relevant information and represent the content of a preposition while still being in an abstract form. For example, the representation can be enriched by annotating the place-holder with the grammatical case of the preposition it represents: for overt prepositions, case is often an indicator of the content (e.g. direction/location), whereas for NPs, case indicates

Proceedings of SSST-9, Ninth Workshop on Syntax, Semantics and Structure in Statistical Translation, pages 55–56,
Denver, Colorado, June 4, 2015.

input	lemmatized SMT output	prep	morph. feat.	inflected	gloss
∅ ⟶	PREP	∅-Acc	–		
what	welch<PWAT>	Acc	Acc.Fem.Sg.Wk	welche	which
role	Rolle<+NN><Fem><Sg>	Acc	Acc.Fem.Sg.Wk	Rolle	role
∅ ⟶	PREP	∅-Nom	–		
the	die<+ART><Def>	Nom	Nom.Masc.Sg.St	der	the
giant	riesig<ADJ>	Nom	Nom.Masc.Sg.Wk	riesige	giant
planet	Planet<+NN><Masc><Sg>	Nom	Nom.Masc.Sg.Wk	Planet	planet
has	gespielt<VVPP>	–	–	gespielt	played
played	hat<VAFIN>	–	–	hat	has
in ⟶	PREP	bei-Dat	–	bei	for
the	die<+ART><Def>	Dat	Dat.Fem.Sg.St	der	the
development	Entwicklung<+NN><Fem><Sg>	Dat	Dat.Fem.Sg.Wk	Entwicklung	development
of ⟶	PREP	∅-Gen	–		
the	die<+ART><Def>	Gen	Gen.Neut.Sg.St	des	of-the
solar system	Sonnensystem<+NN><Neut><Sg>	Gen	Gen.Neut.Sg.Wk	Sonnensystems	solar system

Figure 1: Overview of the morphology-aware translation system: prediction of prepositions, morphological features and generation of inflected forms. German cases: Acc-Accusative, Nom-Nominative, Dat-Dative, Gen-Genitive.

the syntactic function. Other variants contain information of the governing verb/noun, and whether the represented preposition is functional.

For the prediction of prepositions, we combine the following feature types into a linear-chain CRF: *target-side context* (lemmas, POS-tags), *source-side context* (the aligned phrase), *projected source-side information* (relevant target-side words obtained based on source-side parses) and *target-side subcategorizational preferences* (distributional subcategorization information). These features address both functional and content-bearing prepositions, but do not require an explicit distinction between the two categories.

Experiments and Discussion We compare the approach of generating prepositions on the target-side with a morphology-aware SMT system with no special treatment for prepositions. When using "plain" place-holders, there is a considerable drop in BLEU (16.81) in comparison to the baseline (17.38). The annotation of *case* on the place-holders, the best of the abstract representation variants, leads to an improvement (17.23), but still does not surpass the baseline. Additionally, we assess the translation accuracy of prepositions. To allow for an automatic evaluation, we restrict the evaluation to cases where the relevant parts, namely the governing verb and the noun governed by the preposition, are the same in reference and MT output. While there is a minor improvement over the baseline, the difference is very small.

Our approach aims at assigning subcategorized elements to their respective functions and to inflect them accordingly which allows to handle structural differences in source and target language. While the systems fail to improve over the baseline, our experiments show that a meaningful representation of place-holders during translation is a key factor. In particular, the annotation of *case* helps, which can be considered as a "light" semantic annotation. Thus, the addition of more semantically motivated information might lead to a more meaningful representation and remains an interesting idea for future work.

Acknowledgements This project has received funding from the European Union's Horizon 2020 research and innovation programme under grant agreement No 644402, the DFG grants *Distributional Approaches to Semantic Relatedness* and *Models of Morphosyntax for Statistical Machine Translation* and a DFG Heisenberg Fellowship.

References

Eneko Agirre, Aitziber Atutxa, Gorka Labaka, Mikel Lersundi, Aingeru Mayor, and Kepa Sarasola. 2009. Use of Rich Linguistic Information to Translate Prepositions and Grammatical Cases to Basque. In *EAMT*.

Alexander Fraser, Marion Weller, Aoife Cahill, and Fabienne Cap. 2012. Modeling Inflection and Word-Formation in SMT. In *EACL*.

Kristina Toutanova, Hisami Suzuki, and Achim Ruopp. 2008. Applying Morphology Generation Models to Machine Translation. In *ACL*.

Marion Weller, Alexander Fraser, and Sabine Schulte im Walde. 2013. Using Subcategorization Knowledge to Improve Case Prediction for Translation to German. In *ACL*.

Marion Weller, Alexander Fraser, and Sabine Schulte im Walde. 2015. Target-Side Generation of Prepositions for SMT. In *EAMT*.

Translation reranking using source phrase dependency features

Antonio Valerio Miceli-Barone
Dipartimento di Informatica
Largo B. Pontecorvo, 3
56127 Pisa, Italy
miceli@di.unipi.it

Abstract

We describe a N-best reranking model based on features that combine source-side dependency syntactical information and segmentation and alignment information. Specifically, we consider segmentation-aware "phrase dependency" features.

1 Introduction

Dependency features have been used in the past for both direct translation and reranking (Gimpel and Smith, 2013), usually in a string-to-tree or a tree-to-tree configuration. These approaches generally require the decoder to be specifically designed to produce suitable dependency structures on its output, or to use a specialized target-side parser capable of parsing potentially ungrammatical and unidiomatic sentences.

Instead, we investigated a tree-to-string N-best reranking model suitable for use with a standard phrase-based decoder and a standard source-side dependency parser.

2 Source phrase dependency model

Dependency relations in a conventional dependency tree are syntactical relations between individual words. A phrase-based decoder, instead, operates in terms of phrase-pairs.

Each N-best candidate translation e_i of a source sentence f is defined by its derivation, which describes how f has been segmented into source phrases, how these source phrases have been reorederd and for each source phrase which corresponding target phrase has been chosen.

In our model, we focus on the quality of phrase segmentation and reordering.

Segmentation features The source phrases produced by the segmentation performed by the decoder do not necessarily correspond to subtrees in the dependency parse tree (or forest) g_f of the sentence. And if the dependency parse is not projective, subtrees do not necessarily correspond to contiguous phrases in any possible segmentation.

We propose a set of multiple features which operate at source phrase level, inspired by the concept of *phrase dependency* relations of Gimpel and Smith (2013):

Given a source phrase $\bar{f}_j$ in a derivation, we define the set of its parent phrases $PARENTS(\bar{f}_j)$ as the set of other phrases in the same derivation which contain at least one word that is a parent of some word in $\bar{f}_j$. We also define the sets of left parents $PARENTS_L(\bar{f}_j)$, right parents $PARENTS_R(\bar{f}_j)$, left children $CHILDREN_L(\bar{f}_j)$ and right children $CHILDREN_R(\bar{f}_j)$. Note that only word dependency relations that cross the phrase boundaries are relevant to the definition of these phrase dependency relations.

We propose the following segmentation phrase feature functions:

No parents $PARENTS(\bar{f}_j) = \emptyset$, no left par-

Proceedings of SSST-9, Ninth Workshop on Syntax, Semantics and Structure in Statistical Translation, pages 57–60,
Denver, Colorado, June 4, 2015.

ents $PARENTS_L(\bar{f}_j) = \emptyset$, no right parents $PARENTS_R(\bar{f}_j) = \emptyset$, one-sided parents $PARENTS_L(\bar{f}_j) = \emptyset \vee PARENTS_R(\bar{f}_j) = \emptyset$. Unambiguous (no more than one) parents $|PARENTS(\bar{f}_j)| \leq 1$, Unambiguous left parents $|PARENTS_L(\bar{f}_j)| \leq 1$, Unambiguous right parents $|PARENTS_L(\bar{f}_j)| \leq 1$. Unique parent $|PARENTS(\bar{f}_j)| = 1$. No children $CHILDREN(\bar{f}_j) = \emptyset$, no left children $CHILDREN_L(\bar{f}_j) = \emptyset$, no right children $CHILDREN_R(\bar{f}_j) = \emptyset$, one-sided children $CHILDREN_L(\bar{f}_j) = \emptyset \vee CHILDREN_R(\bar{f}_j) = \emptyset$.

When phrase segmentation breaks the syntactic structures these features should be able to detect it, and the model will penalize (or perhaps reward) different types of breakages using parameters automatically learned by tuning, similarly to Cherry (2008) or Marton and Resnik (2008).

Distortion features We consider pairs of source phrases which are aligned to target phrases that are contiguous in target order.

Let $\bar{f}_j \equiv (\bar{f}_{a(j-1)}, \bar{f}_{a(j)})$ be one of such pairs. We define the following, mutually exclusive, feature functions:
Unique parent-child $PARENTS(\bar{f}_{a(j)}) = \{\bar{f}_{a(j-1)}\}$. Unique child-parent $PARENTS(\bar{f}_{a(j-1)}) = \{\bar{f}_{a(j)}\}$. Siblings with unique parent $\exists j' : PARENTS(\bar{f}_{a(j)}) = PARENTS(\bar{f}_{a(j-1)}) = \bar{f}_{j'}$. None of the above.

We also define the inversion feature function $a(j-1) > a(j)$ which is included both as an individual feature and in logical conjunction with each of the feature functions defined above, resulting in a total of nine boolean distortion feature functions.

These features detect reordering operations which swap syntactic structures related by a dependency relation between themselves or with a shared parent structure, similarly to the reordering operations in the *synchronous dependency insertion grammar* of Ding and Palmer (2005) or the *syntactic coupling* features of Nikoulina and Dymetman (2008).

Scoring model The feature functions defined in the two previous paragraphs are combined into a vector which is concatenated to the feature vector produced by the decoder and multiplied by a parameter vector θ to obtain the final reranking score for each candidate translation. θ is trained using a standard machine translation tuning technique, namely K-best batch MIRA (Cherry and Foster, 2012).

3 Experiments

Setup We tested our model in a Italian-to-English 1000-best translation reranking task.

We trained the baseline phrase-based system using a parallel corpus assembled from Europarl v7 (Koehn, 2005), JRC-ACQUIS v2.2 (Steinberger et al., 2006) and additional bilingual articles crawled from online newspaper websites[1], totaling 3,081,700 sentence pairs, which were split into a 3,075,777 sp. phrase-table training corpus, a 3,923 sp. tuning corpus, and a 2,000 sp. test corpus.

We trained and tuned phrase-based Moses (Koehn et al., 2007) using a "sparse features" configuration (the "word translation" and "phrase translation" feature sets described by Chiang et al. (2009)). We performed model parameter tuning using k-best batch MIRA.
Non-projective dependency parse trees (actually, forests) for the Italian source sentences have been computed using the transition-based DeSR parser in tree revision configuration (Attardi and Ciaramita, 2007).

Significance was estimated using *paired bootstrap resampling* (Koehn, 2004).

Results The results of these experiments are shown in fig. 1.

We obtain a small but significant BLUE score improvement.

We also performed other experiments with slightly different feature function configurations but we obtained lower scores, although never lower than the baseline score of the decoder.

From a computational time point of view, the reranker adds a negligible overhead the the

[1]Corriere.it and Asianews.it

Configuration	BLEU-c	BLEU
Moses + sparse feats.	29.02	29.82
Moses + sparse feats. + dep. feats.	29.17 (+ 0.15)	29.97 (+ 0.15)

Figure 1: Experimental results. BLEU and case-insensitive BLEU scores over a 2,000 sp. it-en test corpus. Improvements are significant at the p ¡ 0.05 significance level.

runtime of the decoder, even in our unoptimized Python implementation.

Conclusions and future work We identified a set of syntactic dependency features which can provide small but significant translation quality improvements when used in N-best reranking, at least on the Italian-to-English language pair. We need to perform experiments on other language pairs to determine whether this result generalizes.

Spurious effects due to optimizer instability that can't be detected by our significance tests might be present. More advanced statistical tests such as Clark et al. (2011) should be performed to increase the confidence in the validity of our result.

In addition to reranking, our feature functions could also be used for decoding in a standard phrase-based or hierarchical translation system without a significant increase of decoding complexity, since they decompose additively over phrases or pair of phrase adjacent in target-order. Performing such experiment will be a natural extension of our work.

References

Giuseppe Attardi and Massimiliano Ciaramita. 2007. Tree revision learning for dependency parsing. In Candace L. Sidner, Tanja Schultz, Matthew Stone, and ChengXiang Zhai, editors, *HLT-NAACL*, pages 388–395. The Association for Computational Linguistics.

Colin Cherry and George Foster. 2012. Batch tuning strategies for statistical machine translation. In *Proceedings of the 2012 Conference of the North American Chapter of the Association for Computational Linguistics: Human Language Technologies*, pages 427–436. Association for Computational Linguistics.

Colin Cherry. 2008. Cohesive phrase-based decoding for statistical machine translation. In *In Proceedings of ACL-08: HLT*, pages 72–80.

David Chiang, Kevin Knight, and Wei Wang. 2009. 11,001 new features for statistical machine translation. In *Proceedings of Human Language Technologies: The 2009 Annual Conference of the North American Chapter of the Association for Computational Linguistics*, pages 218–226. Association for Computational Linguistics.

Jonathan H Clark, Chris Dyer, Alon Lavie, and Noah A Smith. 2011. Better hypothesis testing for statistical machine translation: Controlling for optimizer instability. In *Proceedings of the 49th Annual Meeting of the Association for Computational Linguistics: Human Language Technologies: short papers-Volume 2*, pages 176–181. Association for Computational Linguistics.

Yuan Ding and Martha Palmer. 2005. Machine translation using probabilistic synchronous dependency insertion grammars. In *Proceedings of the 43rd Annual Meeting on Association for Computational Linguistics*, ACL '05, pages 541–548, Stroudsburg, PA, USA. Association for Computational Linguistics.

Kevin Gimpel and Noah A Smith. 2013. Phrase dependency machine translation with quasi-synchronous tree-to-tree features.

Philipp Koehn, Hieu Hoang, Alexandra Birch, Chris Callison-Burch, Marcello Federico, Nicola Bertoldi, Brooke Cowan, Wade Shen, Christine Moran, Richard Zens, Chris Dyer, Ondřej Bojar, Alexandra Constantin, and Evan Herbst. 2007. Moses: open source toolkit for statistical machine translation. In *Proceedings of the 45th Annual Meeting of the ACL on Interactive Poster and Demonstration Sessions*, ACL '07, pages 177–180, Stroudsburg, PA, USA. Association for Computational Linguistics.

Philipp Koehn. 2004. Statistical significance tests for machine translation evaluation. In *EMNLP*, pages 388–395.

Philipp Koehn. 2005. Europarl: A parallel corpus for statistical machine translation. In *Conference Proceedings: the tenth Machine Translation Summit*, pages 79–86, Phuket, Thailand. AAMT, AAMT.

Yuval Marton and Philip Resnik. 2008. Soft syntactic constraints for hierarchical phrased-based translation. In *ACL*, pages 1003–1011.

Vassilina Nikoulina and Marc Dymetman. 2008. Using syntactic coupling features for discriminating phrase-based translations (wmt-08 shared translation task). In *Proceedings of the Third Workshop on Statistical Machine Translation*, pages 159–162. Association for Computational Linguistics.

Ralf Steinberger, Bruno Pouliquen, Anna Widiger, Camelia Ignat, Tomaz Erjavec, Dan Tufis, and Dniel Varga. 2006. The jrc-acquis: A multilingual aligned parallel corpus with 20+ languages. In *Proceedings of the 5th International Conference on Language Resources and Evaluation (LREC'2006)*, Genoa, Italy.

Semantics-based pretranslation for SMT using fuzzy matches

Tom Vanallemeersch, Vincent Vandeghinste
Centre for Computational Linguistics
Blijde Inkomststraat 13
B-3000 Leuven, Belgium
{tom,vincent}@ccl.kuleuven.be

Abstract

Semantic knowledge has been adopted recently for SMT preprocessing, decoding and evaluation, in order to be able to compare sentences based on their meaning rather than on mere lexical and syntactic similarity. Little attention has been paid to semantic knowledge in the context of integrating fuzzy matches from a translation memory with SMT. We present work in progress which focuses on semantics-based pretranslation before decoding in SMT. This involves applying fuzzy matching metrics based on lexical semantics and semantic roles, aligning parse trees based on semantic roles, and pretranslating matching source sentence parts using aligned tree nodes.

1 Introduction

Semantic knowledge has been adopted recently for SMT preprocessing, decoding and evaluation. Using such knowledge helps for comparing sentences based on meaning rather than form, and for moving away from the assumption of lexical and syntactic similarity between source and target sentences. Little attention has been paid to semantic knowledge in the context of integrating fuzzy matches with SMT. Fuzzy matching methods were originally designed for translation memories, in which translators store their translations. They are now also being used in the context of SMT, for pretranslating parts of sentences before or during decoding. These methods pretranslate matching sentence parts through word alignment, parse node alignment and phrase tables, and use different degrees of linguistic knowledge.

As far as we know, semantic knowledge has not yet been applied for pretranslating sentence parts before decoding in SMT. Therefore, we would like to present our work in progress, which investigates, on the one hand, the use of semantic knowledge (lexical semantics and semantic roles) for improving the usability of fuzzy matches, and, on the other hand, the pretranslation of matching sentence parts using parse nodes aligned through semantic role information.

In Section 2, we provide background on fuzzy matching and on semantic knowledge in SMT, including our own previous research on fuzzy matching and tree alignment. In Section 3, we provide the methodology we are currently devising for semantics-based pretranslation. As this is work in progress, results are not yet provided. However, the discussion of our recent work on combination of fuzzy matching metrics and on semantics-based tree alignment will hint at the potential of using additional sources of linguistic information, such as lexical semantics and semantic roles, for fuzzy matching.

2 Background

The principle of fuzzy matching in a translation memory can be applied to flat sequences or to trees, and either be applied in a linguistically unaware way or involve some degree of linguistic knowledge. Fuzzy matching may be performed using classical sequence comparison metrics like Levenshtein distance (Levenshtein, 1966) or other metrics specifically designed for fuzzy matching, like the ones of Bloodgood and Strauss (2014). It may also be ap-

Proceedings of SSST-9, Ninth Workshop on Syntax, Semantics and Structure in Statistical Translation, pages 61–64,
Denver, Colorado, June 4, 2015. ©2015 Association for Computational Linguistics

plied using MT evaluation metrics like TER (Snover et al., 2006) and Meteor (Denkowski and Lavie, 2014), which were originally designed to compare MT output with one or more reference translations. In this respect, it should be noted that fuzzy matching is performed at the sub-segment level, as it determines matching parts, while MT evaluation is performed on the segment level (Callison-Burch et al., 2012). However, evaluating MT output at the sub-segment level may also be helpful, for instance to determine whether specific parts are translated better than other ones. As for the quality of fuzzy matching metrics, combined metrics appear to perform better than individual ones. For instance, Vanallemeersch and Vandeghinste (2015) combine linguistically unaware with syntactically oriented metrics using regression trees.

In recent years, there has been increasing interest in integrating fuzzy matches with SMT. An example of a linguistically unaware approach is described by Koehn and Senellart (2010), who pretranslate sentences before decoding, using the word alignment between the matching source sentence in the translation memory and its translation. Instead of using the translation of matched parts for pretranslation, the parts and their translation may also be used for enriching a phrase table, as shown by Simard and Isabelle (2009). An example of a linguistically aware integration approach is described by Zhechev and van Genabith (2010), who pretranslate sentences using the node alignment between the parse trees of the source and target sentences in the translation memory. He et al. (2011) apply linguistic knowledge on matching parts during – instead of before – decoding, for instance semantic knowledge.

As indicated above, pretranslation using fuzzy matching involves word alignment or tree alignment. The latter may be based on syntactic information in the trees, but may also involve semantic roles (Vanallemeersch, 2012). Semantic roles are increasingly being used in SMT, in various ways. For instance, Aziz et al. (2011) and Liu and Gildea (2010) annotate source sentences or parses with semantic roles before training an SMT system, while Wu and Fung (2009) compare the semantic roles in the parse tree of a translation hypothesis with the roles in the source parse tree. As regards MT evaluation using semantic roles, metrics like MEANT (Lo and Wu, 2011) have been developed.

3 Methodology

Below, we explain the methodology we are currently devising for semantic pretranslation. It consists of two steps: a fuzzy matching step which makes use of semantic knowledge (lexical semantics and semantic roles), and a pretranslation step which detects the translation of matching sentence parts through semantics-based node alignment of source and target parse trees.

3.1 Semantics-based fuzzy matching

We apply MT evaluation metrics like Meteor and MEANT to source sentences. Meteor allows for matching using synonyms and paraphrases (lexical semantics), while MEANT focuses on semantic roles. We apply a testing framework for applying metrics to sentences in the source and target language and comparing metrics (Vanallemeersch and Vandeghinste, 2015). The framework takes a leave-one-out approach: each source sentence in the translation memory is compared to all other source sentences in the memory. Given some source sentence X (with translation Y), we select the source sentence X' in the memory which has the highest match score according to a metric, and compare its translation, Y', to Y, the desired translation. The comparison of Y and Y', like the comparison of source sentences, takes place using some similarity metric like TER or MEANT (which we refer to as the *target language metric*).

We compare the performance of linguistically unaware fuzzy matching metrics and syntactically oriented metrics on the one hand with semantically oriented metrics on the other hand. When comparing linguistically unaware to syntactically oriented metrics using the above framework (Vanallemeersch and Vandeghinste, 2015), we noted combined metrics have a greater ability to predict the quality of Y', i.e. they are better at predicting how useful the target language metric will consider Y' for translating X. Therefore, we expect that combining a semantically oriented fuzzy matching metric with other types of metrics will lead to better predictions than using the metric in isolation. We also investigate the relation between source language and target language metrics (using the same metric in both languages may favour the source language metric over other ones). Therefore, it may be interesting to make use of human judgments of matches. However, as human evaluation is labour-intensive, and the final use of the matches lies in the integration with SMT, it may be more interesting to focus attention to the evaluation of the MT output produced after the pretranslation step described in section 3.2.

We primarily focus on the language pair English-Dutch. When applying Meteor and MEANT to English sentences, we make use of resources such as the set of English paraphrases in Meteor and the syntactic-semantic parser of Johansson and Nugues (2008), which assigns PropBank and Nombank labels (Palmer et al., 2005; Meyers et al., 2004). For Dutch, we make use of our semantic role labeler described in section 3.2 and of a Dutch paraphrase set created from English-Dutch Moses phrase tables (Koehn et al., 2003) using the *parex* tool (Denkowski and Lavie, 2010; Bannard and Callison-Burch, 2005).

3.2 Semantics-based pretranslation

Applying tree alignment in order to link nodes between source and parse trees (Zhechev and van Genabith, 2010) allows for making use of syntactic information during fuzzy matching. However, the semantic load of a sentence may be expressed in different syntactic ways, leading to possibly different syntactic structures in a source and parse tree. As an example, a source sentence may contain an structure with an active verb and its translation a structure with a passive verb, leading the semantic load to be identical, but the syntactic structure to be different. Another example is a sentence pair in which an English deverbal noun (say, *judgment*) corresponds to a Dutch verb (*beoordelen*). Therefore, we perform tree alignment based on predicates and semantic roles rather than syntactic information. To this effect, we apply semantic role labelers to source and target parses in the translation memory and align the nodes of the resulting parses using a combination of semantic information and lexical probabilities from SMT.

A Dutch semantic role labeler trained on manually annotated data which is able to identify both verbal and nominal predicates does not exist yet; the labeler used in the SoNaR project (Schuurman et al., 2010) only identifies verbal predicates. Therefore, we apply crosslingual projection from English source to Dutch target trees, parsed with Alpino (van Noord, 2006), and train a semantic role labeler for Dutch based on the target trees with projected information (Vanallemeersch, 2012). This approach for training a labeler does not require manual intervention.

After applying a fuzzy matching metric to a source sentence to be translated, we select the best match in the translation memory, and apply a procedure similar to the one of Zhechev and Van Genabith (2010): we find out the translation of the matching source parts by detecting the source nodes overlapping with these parts and retrieving the tokens dominated by the aligned target nodes. In the input to the SMT system, we mark up the source parts with the target tokens, which allows the SMT system to make use of the tokens during decoding. We evaluate the SMT output produced using semantics-based pretranslation through an MT evaluation metric such as MEANT, and compare the SMT output to the one obtained with pretranslation based on mere word alignment or on syntax-based tree alignment.

Acknowledgments

This research is funded by the Flemish government agency IWT (project 130041, SCATE). See http://www.ccl.kuleuven.be/scate.

References

Wilker Aziz, Miguel Rios, and Lucia Specia. 2011. Shallow semantic trees for SMT. *Proceedings of the Sixth Workshop on Statistical Machine Translation, Edinburgh, Scotland, July 30–31*, pp. 316–322.

Colin Bannard and Chris Callison-Burch. 2005. Paraphrasing with Bilingual Parallel Corpora. *Proceedings of the 43rd Annual Meeting of the Association for Computational Linguistics, Ann Arbor, Michigan, USA, June 25–30*, pp. 597–604.

Michael Bloodgood and Benjamin Strauss. 2014. Translation memory retrieval methods. *Proceedings of the 14th Conference of the European Association for Computational Linguistics, Gothenburg, Sweden, April 26–30*, pp. 202–210.

Chris Callison-Burch, Philipp Koehn, Christof Monz, Matt Post, Radu Soricut, and Lucia Specia. 2012. Findings of the 2012 Workshop on Statistical Machine Translation. *Proceedings of the Seventh Workshop on Statistical Machine Translation, Montréal, Canada, June 7–8*, pp. 10–51.

Michael Denkowski and Alon Lavie. 2010. METEOR-NEXT and the METEOR Paraphrase Tables: Improved Evaluation Support For Five Target Languages. *Proceedings of the ACL 2010 Joint Workshop on Statistical Machine Translation and Metrics MATR, Uppsala, Sweden, July 15–16*, pp. 339–342.

Michael Denkowski and Alon Lavie. 2014. Meteor Universal: Language Specic Translation Evaluation for Any Target Language. *Proceedings of the Ninth Workshop on Statistical Machine Translation, Baltimore, Maryland, USA, June 26–27*, pp. 376–380.

Yifan He, Yanjun Ma, Andy Way, and Josef van Genabith. 2011. Rich Linguistic Features for Translation Memory-Inspired Consistent Translation. *Proceedings of MT Summit XIII, Xiamen, China, September 19–23*, pp. 456–463.

Richard Johansson and Pierre Nugues. 2008. Dependency-based Semantic Role Labeling of PropBank. *Proceedings of the Conference on Empirical Methods in Natural Language Processing, Waikiki, Honolulu, Hawaii, USA, October 25-27*, pp. 69–78.

Philipp Koehn, Franz Josef Och, and Daniel Marcu. 2003. Statistical Phrase-based Translation. *Proceedings of the 2003 Conference of the North American Chapter of the Association for Computational Linguistics on Human Language Technology - Volume 1, Edmonton, Canada, May 27 – June 1*, pp. 48–54.

Philipp Koehn and Jean Senellart. 2010. Convergence of Translation Memory and Statistical Machine Translation. *Proceedings of AMTA Workshop on MT Research and the Translation Industry, Denver, Colorado, USA, November 4*, pp. 21–31.

Vladimir I. Levenshtein. 1966. Binary codes capable of correcting deletions, insertions, and reversals. *Soviet Physics Doklady*, 10(8):707–710.

Ding Liu and Daniel Gildea. 2010. Semantic role features for machine translation. *Proceedings of the 23rd International Conference on Computational Linguistics, Beijing, China, August 23–27*, pp. 716–724.

Chi-kiu Lo and Dekai Wu. 2011. MEANT: an inexpensive, high-accuracy, semi-automatic metric for evaluating translation utility via semantic frames. *Proceedings of the 49th Annual Meeting of the Association for Computational Linguistics: Human Language Technologies - Volume 1, Portland, Oregon, USA, June 19–24*, pp. 220–229.

Adam Meyers, Ruth Reeves, Catherine Macleod, Rachel Szekely, Veronika Zielinska, Brian Young, and Ralph Grishman. 2004. Annotating Noun Argument Structure for NomBank. *Proceedings of LREC-2004, Lisbon, Portugal, May 26–28*, pp. 803–806.

Martha Palmer, Daniel Gildea, and Paul Kingsbury. 2005. The Proposition Bank: An Annotated Corpus of Semantic Roles. *Computational Linguistics*, 31(1):71–106.

Ineke Schuurman, Véronique Hoste, and Paola Monachesi. 2010. Interacting semantic layers of annotation in SoNaR, a reference corpus of contemporary written Dutch. *Proceedings of the Seventh conference on international language resources and evaluation, Valletta, Malta, May 17–23*, pp. 2471–2477.

Michel Simard and Pierre Isabelle. 2009. Phrase-based machine translation in a computer-assisted translation environment. *Proceedings of MT Summit XII, Ottawa, Ontario, Canada, August 26–30*, pp. 120–127.

Matthew Snover, Bonnie Dorr, Richard Schwartz, Linnea Micciulla, and John Makhoul. 2006. A study of translation edit rate with targeted human annotation. *Proceedings of the Seventh Conference of the Association for Translation in the Americas, Cambridge, Massachusetts, USA, August 8–12*, pp. 223–231.

Tom Vanallemeersch. 2012. Parser-independent Semantic Tree Alignment. *Proceedings of META-RESEARCH Workshop on Advanced Treebanking, in conjunction with LREC-2012, Istanbul, Turkey, May 22*, pp. 1–5.

Tom Vanallemeersch and Vincent Vandeghinste. 2015 [accepted]. Assessing linguistically aware fuzzy matching in translation memories. *Proceedings of the 18th Annual Conference of EAMT, Antalya, Turkey, May 11–13*.

Gertjan van Noord. 2006. At Last Parsing Is Now Operational. *Proceedings of TALN 2006, Leuven, Belgium, April 10–13*, pp. 20–42.

Dekai Wu and Pascale Fung. 2009. Semantic roles for SMT: a hybrid two-pass model. *Proceedings of Human Language Technologies: The 2009 Annual Conference of the North American Chapter of the Association for Computational Linguistics, Companion Volume: Short Papers, Boulder, Colorado, USA*, pp. 13–16.

Ventsislav Zhechev and Josef van Genabith. 2010. Maximising TM performance through sub-tree alignment and SMT. *Proceedings of the Ninth conference of the Association for Machine Translation in the Americas, Denver, Colorado, USA, October 31 – November 4*, http://www.mt-archive.info/AMTA-2010-Zhechev.pdf.

What Matters Most in Morphologically Segmented SMT Models?

Mohammad Salameh[†] **Colin Cherry**[‡] **Grzegorz Kondrak**[†]

[†]Department of Computing Science
University of Alberta
Edmonton, AB, T6G 2E8, Canada
{msalameh,gkondrak}@ualberta.ca

[‡]National Research Council Canada
1200 Montreal Road
Ottawa, ON, K1A 0R6, Canada
Colin.Cherry@nrc-cnrc.gc.ca

Abstract

Morphological segmentation is an effective strategy for addressing difficulties caused by morphological complexity. In this study, we use an English-to-Arabic test bed to determine what steps and components of a phrase-based statistical machine translation pipeline benefit the most from segmenting the target language. We test several scenarios that differ primarily in when desegmentation is applied, showing that the most important criterion for success in segmentation is to allow the system to build target words from morphemes that span phrase boundaries. We also investigate the impact of segmented and unsegmented target language models (LMs) on translation quality. We show that an unsegmented LM is helpful according to BLEU score, but also leads to a drop in the overall usage of compositional morphology, bringing it to well below the amount observed in human references.

1 Introduction

It is well known that morphological segmentation can improve statistical machine translation (SMT). By splitting relevant morphological affixes into independent tokens, segmentation has repeatedly been shown to improve translation into or out of morphologically complex languages. Segmentation as a preprocessing step brings several benefits to translation:

- **Correspondence** with morphologically simple languages, such as English is improved. In Figure 1, segmenting *bsyArth* allows one-to-one links for "with", "his" and "car".

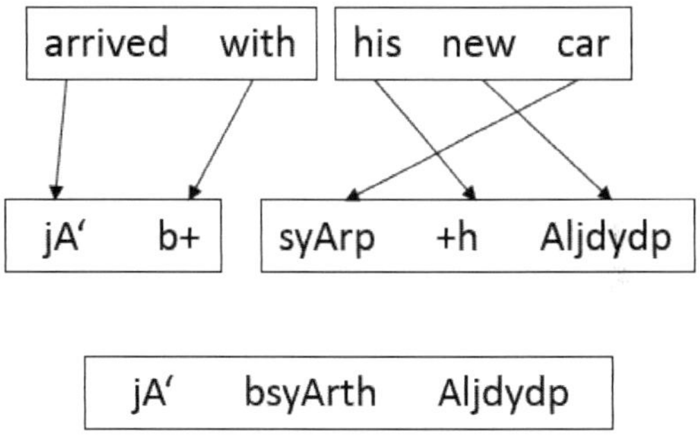

Figure 1: An illustration of one-to-one correspondence between Arabic morphemes and English words. Arabic text is segmented using the PATB tokenization scheme, and shown in Buckwalter transliteration.

- By building models over morphemes, rather than words, **data sparsity** is reduced.
- By allowing morphemes with clear syntactic roles to be translated independently, we increase our **expressive power** by creating new lexical translations. For example, using the two phrase-pairs in Figure 1 results in a new word after desegmentation (b+ syArp +h $\Rightarrow$ bsyArth), which might not have existed in the training data.

However, there is also a price to be paid. While morpheme-level models are more resistant to data sparsity, they account for less context than word-level models, make stronger independence assumptions, and they are less efficient statistically, in that they devote probability mass to sequences containing illegal words. Furthermore, when segmentation is applied to the target language, the process must be

Proceedings of SSST-9, Ninth Workshop on Syntax, Semantics and Structure in Statistical Translation, pages 65–73,
Denver, Colorado, June 4, 2015.

reversed at the end of the pipeline to present the output in a readable format. This **desegmentation** step complicates our pipeline, and can introduce errors.

Our work is inspired by two recent contributions that attempt to combine the advantages of word- and morpheme-based models. Luong et al. (2010) combine word and morpheme views in a desegmented phrase table, allowing morphemes to reduce sparsity while words expand context, and eliminating the need for a separate desegmentation step. Their word-boundary-aware morpheme-level phrase extraction technique restricts phrase boundaries so that no target phrase can begin with a suffix or end with a prefix. This allows them to desegment each target phrase independently, enabling the use of both word- and morpheme-level language models during decoding. However, this phrase-table desegmentation approach lacks the expressive power that comes from translating morphemes independently.

More recently, Salameh et al. (2014) propose a lattice desegmentation approach, which comes close to combining all the advantages of word and morpheme views. By desegmenting a lattice that compactly represents many translation options, and rescoring it with a word-level language model, they avoid restricting the phrase table. However, by delaying desegmentation until rescoring, the approach loses Luong et al. (2010)'s advantage of full decoder integration.

In this paper, we present an experimental study of English-to-Arabic translation that is designed to better understand the impact of various trade-offs when translating into a morphologically segmented target language, and to identify what aspects of segmentation are most beneficial to translation. The benefits of segmentation can impact several components in the SMT pipeline: the alignment model, the translation table, and the various language and translation models. Throughout this study, we investigate the effect of varying the point in the SMT pipeline where the segmentation is reversed. In addition, we attempt to combine word- and morpheme-level models within the decoder as much as possible.

Our experimental study provides three novel insights. First, we present strong evidence indicating that the ability to build target words across phrase boundaries is the most important property of target language segmentation. This implies that phrase table desegmentation, the only published desegmentation technique that has been fully integrated into decoding, gives up segmentation's primary advantage. Second, we draw a previously unobserved connection between the use of an unsegmented LM and the decoder's overall use of compositional morphology; we show that although unsegmented LMs tend to increase BLEU score, they also reduce the system's use of morphological affixes to well below that of a human. Finally, we present the first direct comparison between phrase table desegmentation (Luong et al., 2010) and lattice desegmentation (Salameh et al., 2014).

2 Background

Our work builds on earlier studies of automatic morphological segmentation and its impact on SMT. There are many ways to segment syntactically relevant affixes from stems. Supervised techniques may either pass through an intermediate morphological analysis (Habash et al., 2009), or directly segment the character stream (Green and DeNero, 2012); recent work on supervised Arabic segmentation focuses primarily on adaptation to dialects (Habash et al., 2013; Monroe et al., 2014). There are also a host of unsupervised techniques (Creutz and Lagus, 2005; Lee et al., 2011; Sirts and Goldwater, 2013), which provide valuable language portability, but which generally fall behind supervised methods when labeled data is available.

There is a large body of work studying the best form of segmentation when translating from a morphologically complex source language (Sadat and Habash, 2006; Stallard et al., 2012), where the segmentation can be used as a simple preprocessing step, or to create an input lattice (Dyer et al., 2008). Recently, there has been a growing interest in segmentation on the target side (Oflazer and Durgar El-Kahlout, 2007), which introduces a question of how to perform proper desegmentation (Badr et al., 2008). El Kholy and Habash (2012) have conducted a thorough exploration of the various segmentation and desegmentation options for English to Arabic translation, and we follow their work when designing our test bed.

Method	Unsegmented	Alignment Deseg.	Phrase Table Deseg.	One-best Deseg.	Lattice Deseg.
Desegment before:	Never segment	Phrase extraction	Decoding	Evaluation	Evaluation
Alignment model	Word	Morph	Morph	Morph	Morph
Lexical weights	Word	Word	Morph	Morph	Morph
Language model	Word	Word	Word	Morph	Morph + Word
Tuning	Word	Word	Word	Morph	Morph then Word
Flexible boundaries?	No	No	No	Yes	Yes

Table 1: Desegmentation scenarios and their effect on the components of a typical SMT system.

3 Methods

When translating into a segmented target language, such as Arabic, the segmentation will need to eventually be reversed for the output to be readable. The key insight driving our experiments is that by varying the point in the SMT pipeline where this reversal occurs, we can alter which models are based on morphemes and which are based on words, and thereby determine which components most benefit from segmentation. We assume a phrase-based SMT architecture similar to that of Moses (Koehn et al., 2007), but most of our observations hold for hierarchical and tree-based models. In all of our approaches, we desegment using a mapping table that counts the segmentations performed on the target side of our training data. The table uses counts of word-segmentation pairs to map each morpheme sequence back to its most likely unsegmented word form. We back off to manually crafted rules in cases where the segmented form does not exist in the mapping table (El Kholy and Habash, 2012).

Table 1 summarizes the effect of the desegmentation point on the components of a typical SMT system, indicating which components are built using morphemes and which are built using words. Most components should be familiar, but the last row introduces **flexible boundaries**, a concept that will be central to our study. This property of the phrase table indicates whether phrases can have unattached affixes at their left or right boundaries. Systems without flexible boundaries cannot combine morphemes across phrases to create translations that were not already seen in the parallel text; as such, this property has a large impact on a system's expressive power.

We describe our comparison systems in turn, each corresponding to a column in Table 1. We also describe a segmented language model feature, which can be added to any system that uses a word-level phrase table.

3.1 Baselines

We rely on two main baselines to evaluate what matters most in segmented models. An **unsegmented** system leaves the Arabic target unsegmented and uses an unsegmented language model. This model suffers from data sparsity and poor English-Arabic word correspondence. The decoder always outputs morphologically correct Arabic words, as it does not require a desegmentation step.

Meanwhile, **one-best desegmentation** segments the Arabic target language before training begins, and the decoder's output is generated in segmented form. As a post-processing step, the one-best output is desegmented using a mapping table and desegmentation rules. All of the component models used during decoding are based on morphemes instead of words. The segmented models are intended to help alleviate data sparsity and improve token correspondence. Unlike the unsegmented system, this system requires a desegmentation step, which can produce morphologically incorrect words.

3.2 Alignment Desegmentation

Our unsupervised alignment models (Brown et al., 1993; Och and Ney, 2003) are sensitive both to poor word-to-word correspondence and to data sparsity issues. They are also at the very start of the SMT pipeline; they impact nearly all other downstream models. Therefore, it would be reasonable to suspect that the primary benefit of segmentation could come from improved word alignment. Alignment desegmentation allows us to test this theory by desegmenting immediately after alignment.

More specifically, we segment the target side as pre-processing. After word alignment, we replace the segmented Arabic training data with its unsegmented form. Note that this desegmentation is perfect, as we can always refer to the original sentence to resolve any ambiguities. This is accompanied by desegmenting alignment links by replacing each morpheme index with the index of the unsegmented word that now contains the morpheme. As one would expect, this leads to an increase in the number of one-to-many alignments. Training is then resumed with these links and the unsegmented target. Other than having its alignment model benefit from segmentation, this system has the same properties of an unsegmented system: all remaining component models are based on words. Since all morphemes are desegmented well before decoding begins, it clearly cannot use flexible boundaries to build new words.

3.3 Phrase Table Desegmentation

Our next desegmentation point is after phrase extraction, resulting in a system where we segment the text, align the morphemes, perform phrase extraction over morphemes, and then desegment the resulting tables. Following Luong et al. (2010), we first remove all phrases that have target sides with flexible boundaries, which allows us to desegment each remaining target phrase independently. The result is a desegmented phase table. Note that we leave the various scores associated with each phrase-pair unchanged.

This model is similar to alignment desegmentation described in the previous section in that all remaining components and operations are based on words. However, there are two key differences. First, the lexical weights of each phrase are calculated over morphemes rather than words. Second, the phrase-length limit is applied at the morpheme level rather than at the word level. We use this scenario to test the utility of morpheme-level lexical weights.

This system is related to, but not identical to the work of Luong et al. (2010). Their system actually merges tables from an unsegmented model with those from phrase table desegmentation; they investigate a number of methods to combine the scores across tables. In addition, they incorporate both segmented and unsegmented language models, which is a difference that we address in the next section.

3.4 Segmented LM Scoring in Desegmented Models

Both alignment desegmentation and phrase table desegmentation rely on an unsegmented language model, as they naturally decode directly into a desegmented target language. We experiment with augmenting both of these systems with an extra feature: a segmented language model. For each Arabic target word, we add its segmented form to the phrase table as an extra factor (Koehn and Hoang, 2007). We insert this factor after phrase extraction, so it has no impact on alignment or the calculation of translation model scores. The factor merely gives us access to the segmented morphemes during decoding. The decoder uses this factor to apply a segmented language model during each hypothesis extension.

Although the segmented language model spans a shorter context, its scores benefit from the reduced data sparsity that comes from modeling morphemes. In particular, it can unveil whether attaching two hypotheses is grammatical. For example, the unsegmented language model score for the consecutive target phrases [kl m$AklnA] *"all our problems"* [wxlAfAtnA] *"and conflicts"* is relatively low. Scoring their segmented representation [kl m$Akl +nA] [w+ xlAfAt +nA] leads to a more optimistic score, as the segmented language model assesses the morpheme sequence using 4-grams and trigrams, while the unsegmented model scores the word sequence with unigrams and bigrams.

3.5 Lattice Desegmentation

We re-implement the Lattice Desegmentation technique proposed by Salameh et al. (2014), and place it in Table 1 for reference. A system built entirely over morphemes outputs a pruned lattice that compactly represents its hypothesis space. This lattice is then desegmented by composing it with a finite state transducer that maps morpheme sequences into words. By rescoring the desegmented lattice with new features, the system benefits from having both a segmented and desegmented view of the search space. The added features include discontiguity features, as well as an unsegmented language model. The discontiguity features indicate whether a desegmented word came from one contiguous morpheme sequence, two discontiguous sequences, or more.

4 Experimental Setup

We train our English-to-Arabic system using 1.49 million sentence pairs drawn from the NIST 2012 training set, excluding the UN data. This training set contains about 40 million Arabic tokens before segmentation, and 47 million after segmentation. We tune on the NIST 2004 evaluation set (1353 sentences) and evaluate on NIST 2005 (1056 sentences). We also report a second test, which tunes on the NIST 2006 evaluation set (1664 sentences) and evaluates on NIST 2008 (1360 sentences) and 2009 (1313 sentences). NIST 2004 and 2005 datasets have sentences from newswire, while NIST 2006/2008/2009 have sentences drawn from newswire and the web. These evaluation sets are intended for Arabic-to-English translation, and therefore have multiple English references. As we are translating into Arabic, we select the first English reference to use as our source text, and use the Arabic source as our single reference translation.

4.1 Segmentation

For Arabic, morphological segmentation is performed by MADA 3.2 (Habash et al., 2009), using the Penn Arabic Treebank (PATB) segmentation scheme as recommended by El Kholy and Habash (2012). For both segmented and unsegmented Arabic, we further normalize the script by converting different forms of Alif and Ya to bare Alif and dotless Ya. In order to generate the desegmentation table, we analyze the MADA segmentations from the Arabic side of the parallel training data to collect mappings from morpheme sequences to surface forms.

4.2 Systems

We align the parallel data with GIZA++ (Och et al., 2003) and decode using Moses (Koehn et al., 2007). The decoder's log-linear model includes a standard feature set. Four translation model features encode phrase translation probabilities and lexical weights in both directions. Seven distortion features encode a standard distortion penalty as well as a bidirectional lexicalized reordering model. A KN-smoothed 5-gram language model is trained on the target side of the parallel data with SRILM (Stolcke, 2002). Finally, we include word and phrase penalties. The decoder uses Moses' default search parameters, except that the maximum phrase length is set to 8. The decoder's log-linear model is tuned with MERT (Och, 2003). Following Salameh et al. (2014), the tuning of the re-ranking models for lattice desegmentation is performed using a lattice variant of hope-fear MIRA (Cherry and Foster, 2012); lattices are pruned to a density of 50 edges per word before re-ranking. We evaluate our system using BLEU (Papineni et al., 2002).

5 Results

Table 2 shows the results of our translation quality experiments. In previous sections, we mentioned several factors that might contribute to the quality improvements found with segmented models. Beyond the raw ranking of systems, we can use the commonalities and differences between these systems to draw some broad conclusions of what aspects of a segmented system are most important.

5.1 Decoder Integration

Lattice Desegmentation performs best overall, which is not entirely surprising, as it has access to all of the information present in the other systems. Notably, it outperforms Phrase Table Desegmentation; this is the first time to our knowledge that the two have been compared directly.

The main disadvantage of Lattice Deseg, which is not present in Alignment and Phrase Table Deseg, is the lack of decoder integration of its unsegmented view of the target; instead, it is handled by re-ranking a lattice in post-processing. In fact, the top two systems, Lattice Deseg and 1-Best Deseg, are also the only two systems without access to unsegmented information in the decoder. This suggests that the benefits of decoder integration are not sufficient to overcome the trade-offs currently demanded by integration.

5.2 Flexible Boundaries

What is perhaps more surprising is that neither Alignment Deseg nor Phrase Table Deseg are able to match the 1-best Deseg scenario. With the benefit of added segmented language models, both of these systems have access to almost all 1-best Deseg's information and more, yet they fail to match

Model	mt05	mt08	mt09
Unsegmented	32.8	15.0	19.0
Alignment Deseg.	33.4	15.4	19.1
with Segmented LM	33.7	15.4	19.4
Phrase Table Deseg.	33.4	15.5	19.3
with Segmented LM	33.6	15.6	19.7
1-best Deseg.	33.7	15.7	20.2
without flexible boundaries	32.9	15.4	19.4
Lattice Deseg.	34.3	16.4	20.5

Table 2: BLEU scores on on each of the methods described in section 3 . MT05 results are tuned using NIST MT04. Results on NIST MT08 and MT09 datasets are tuned on MT06 dataset.

its translation quality in every test. What both systems lack with respect to 1-best Deseg is flexible phrase boundaries, which allow the creation of new translations across phrases. To confirm the importance of flexible boundaries, we created a new version of 1-best Deseg by pruning all phrases with flexible boundaries from the phrase table, and then re-tuning. The resulting system loses 0.6 BLEU on average, which is more than half of the 0.9 difference between Unsegmented and 1-best Deseg. We conclude that flexible boundaries are one of the most important aspects of a segmentation scenario.

5.3 Language Models

Both Align Deseg and Phrase Table Deseg show consistent, albeit small, improvements from the addition of a segmented LM. In order to assess the importance of the unsegmented LM, we consider 1-best Deseg without flexible boundaries, and Phrase Table Deseg with Segmented LM. These two systems have exactly the same output space, as their respective phrase tables are constructed from morpheme-level phrase extraction followed by pruning flexible boundaries. Furthermore, both systems use a segmented LM and lexical weights built over morphemes. Their only differences are that Phrase Table Deseg uses an unsegmented LM and unsegmented tuning, resulting in BLEU scores that are higher by 0.4 on average. Similarly, a unsegmented LM is one of the main differences between Lattice Deseg and 1-best Deseg, with the others being unsegmented tuning and discontiguity features. Although we have not isolated the unsegmented LM perfectly, these results indicate that it is valuable.

5.4 Lexical Weights

The primary difference between Alignment Deseg and Phrase Table Deseg is that the latter uses morpheme-level lexical weights.[1] Without a segmented LM, we see a 0.1 average BLEU advantage for Phrase Table Deseg, increasing to 0.2 when a segmented LM is included. Unfortunately, these improvements are not consistent across test sets. This suggests that there may be an advantage from morpheme-based lexical weights, but it is certainly not large.

6 Analysis

Our translation quality comparison indicates that flexible boundaries are the most important property of a target segmentation scenario, so we examined them in greater detail. Phrase pairs with flexible boundaries account for roughly 12% of phrases used in the final output of our 1-Best Deseg system.

We performed a detailed analysis to see if the flexible boundaries were used to produce novel words; that is, words that were not seen in the target side of the training data. Roughly 3% of the desegmented types generated by the 1-best-desegmentation system are novel. We randomly selected 40 novel words from each test set to analyze manually. First, none of these desegmented words appear in the reference, and therefore, they have no positive impact on BLEU. Furthermore, 64 of the 120 selected words violate the morphological rules of Arabic. Looking instead at the novel words in the reference, only 115

[1]The other difference is the calculation of the phrase length limit, which favors Alignment Deseg, as its word-based limit allows more phrases overall.

Model	mt05	mt08	mt09
Reference	15.9%	18.1%	18.9%
Unsegmented	12.0%	12.2%	12.6%
Alignment Deseg.	11.6%	11.0%	11.8%
with Segmented LM	11.7%	11.2%	12.0%
Phrase Table Deseg.	11.3%	10.1%	11.2%
with Segmented LM	11.6%	10.5%	11.4%
1-best Deseg.	16.1%	18.2%	19.2%
without flexible boundaries	14.2%	14.7%	15.4%
Lattice Deseg.	10.0%	11.5%	12.2%

Table 3: Percentage of words in the SMT output that have non-identity morphological segmentations.

reference words could not be found in the Arabic side of our training data. Of these, only 37 could be could be constructed from morphemes found in our training set. This means that there is only a small number of opportunities to better match the reference by producing a novel word. Together, these two pieces of analysis strongly suggest that the advantage of flexible boundaries comes from creating new translation options for a given source sequence, rather than from creating novel words.

We were able to compute statistics on flexible boundaries for only two of our systems, because the other three disallow them entirely. In order to characterize all five systems, along with the human references, we measured overall affix usage by counting decomposable words. Table 3 shows the percentage of words in the Arabic translations that have non-identity morphological segmentations when processed by MADA. In terms of affix usage, the 1-best Deseg method tracks the Reference very closely, while all remaining scenarios show a substantial drop in usage of decomposable words. Most surprisingly, Lattice Deseg is included in this group, even though its BLEU scores are higher than 1-best Deseg. Since 1-Best Deseg's most prominent characteristic is its lack of an unsegmented LM, this suggests that unsegmented LMs may dramatically impact affix usage. Note that flexible boundaries do not (fully) account for the gap in affix usage, as the 1-best Deseg still has noticeably higher usage of decomposable words, even with flexible boundaries removed. This implies that Lattice Deseg and the various fully integrated desegmentations could be improved by attempting to directly manipulate their usage of decomposable words, perhaps through a specialized feature.

As a final piece of analysis, we also investigated the impact of different n-gram orders for segmented LMs. Most of the scenarios proposed here add an unsegmented LM to a segmented system, and the most obvious advantage of an unsegmented LM is that it accounts for more context than a segmented LM. However, this only holds if we force both LMs to have the same n-gram order. To see if higher order segmented LMs would improve translation, we experimented with different n-gram orders for our 1-best Deseg system. As we increased the segmented n-gram order from 5 to 8, we saw no improvement over the 5-gram LM used throughout this paper. In fact, BLEU score began to drop after $n = 6$. This suggests that the advantage of adding an unsegmented LM cannot be emulated by increasing the order of the segmented LM.

7 Conclusion

We have presented an experimental study on translation into segmented target languages by creating models that apply desegmentation at different points in the translation pipeline. We have provided evidence that access to phrases with flexible boundaries is a crucial property for a successful segmentation approach. We have also examined the impact of unsegmented LMs, showing that although they are helpful according to BLEU, they also hinder the generation of morphologically-complex words. This suggests that current methods could be improved by attempting to increase their use of morphological affixes.

References

Ibrahim Badr, Rabih Zbib, and James Glass. 2008. Segmentation for English-to-Arabic statistical machine translation. In *Proceedings of ACL*, pages 153–156.

Peter F Brown, Vincent J Della Pietra, Stephen A Della Pietra, and Robert L Mercer. 1993. The mathematics of statistical machine translation: Parameter estimation. *Computational linguistics*, 19(2):263–311.

Colin Cherry and George Foster. 2012. Batch tuning strategies for statistical machine translation. In *Proceedings of HLT-NAACL*, Montreal, Canada, June.

Mathias Creutz and Krista Lagus. 2005. Inducing the morphological lexicon of a natural language from unannotated text. In *In Proceedings of the International and Interdisciplinary Conference on Adaptive Knowledge Representation and Reasoning (AKRR05*, pages 106–113.

Christopher Dyer, Smaranda Muresan, and Philip Resnik. 2008. Generalizing word lattice translation. In *Proceedings of ACL-08: HLT*, pages 1012–1020, Columbus, Ohio, June.

Ahmed El Kholy and Nizar Habash. 2012. Orthographic and morphological processing for English—Arabic statistical machine translation. *Machine Translation*, 26(1-2):25–45, March.

Spence Green and John DeNero. 2012. A class-based agreement model for generating accurately inflected translations. In *Proceedings of the 50th Annual Meeting of the Association for Computational Linguistics (Volume 1: Long Papers)*, pages 146–155, Jeju Island, Korea, July.

Nizar Habash, Owen Rambow, and Ryan Roth. 2009. Mada+tokan: A toolkit for Arabic tokenization, diacritization, morphological disambiguation, POS tagging, stemming and lemmatization. In Khalid Choukri and Bente Maegaard, editors, *Proceedings of the Second International Conference on Arabic Language Resources and Tools*, Cairo, Egypt, April. The MEDAR Consortium.

Nizar Habash, Ryan Roth, Owen Rambow, Ramy Eskander, and Nadi Tomeh. 2013. Morphological analysis and disambiguation for dialectal arabic. In *Proceedings of the 2013 Conference of the North American Chapter of the Association for Computational Linguistics: Human Language Technologies*, pages 426–432, Atlanta, Georgia, June.

Philipp Koehn and Hieu Hoang. 2007. Factored translation models. In *Proceedings of the 2007 Joint Conference on Empirical Methods in Natural Language Processing and Computational Natural Language Learning (EMNLP-CoNLL)*, pages 868–876, Prague, Czech Republic, June.

Philipp Koehn, Hieu Hoang, Alexandra Birch, Chris Callison-Burch, Marcello Federico, Nicola Bertoldi, Brooke Cowan, Wade Shen, Christine Moran, Richard Zens, Chris Dyer, Ondrej Bojar, Alexandra Constantin, and Evan Herbst. 2007. Moses: Open source toolkit for statistical machine translation. In *Proceedings of the 45th Annual Meeting of the Association for Computational Linguistics Companion Volume Proceedings of the Demo and Poster Sessions*, pages 177–180, Prague, Czech Republic, June.

Yoong Keok Lee, Aria Haghighi, and Regina Barzilay. 2011. Modeling syntactic context improves morphological segmentation. In *Proceedings of the Fifteenth Conference on Computational Natural Language Learning*, pages 1–9, Portland, Oregon, USA, June.

Minh-Thang Luong, Preslav Nakov, and Min-Yen Kan. 2010. A hybrid morpheme-word representation for machine translation of morphologically rich languages. In *Proceedings of the 2010 Conference on Empirical Methods in Natural Language Processing*, pages 148–157, Cambridge, MA, October.

Will Monroe, Spence Green, and Christopher D. Manning. 2014. Word segmentation of informal arabic with domain adaptation. In *Proceedings of the 52nd Annual Meeting of the Association for Computational Linguistics (Volume 2: Short Papers)*, pages 206–211, Baltimore, Maryland, June.

Franz Josef Och and Hermann Ney. 2003. A systematic comparison of various statistical alignment models. *Computational linguistics*, 29(1):19–51.

Franz Josef Och, Hermann Ney, Franz Josef, and Och Hermann Ney. 2003. A systematic comparison of various statistical alignment models. *Computational Linguistics*, 29.

Franz Joseph Och. 2003. Minimum error rate training for statistical machine translation. In *Proceedings of ACL*, pages 160–167.

Kemal Oflazer and Ilknur Durgar El-Kahlout. 2007. Exploring different representational units in English-to-Turkish statistical machine translation. In *Proceedings of the Second Workshop on Statistical Machine Translation*, pages 25–32, Prague, Czech Republic, June.

Kishore Papineni, Salim Roukos, Todd Ward, and Wei jing Zhu. 2002. BLEU: a method for automatic evaluation of machine translation. In *Proceedings of 40th Annual Meeting of the Association for Computational Linguistics*, pages 311–318.

Fatiha Sadat and Nizar Habash. 2006. Combination of Arabic preprocessing schemes for statistical machine translation. In *Proceedings of the 21st International Conference on Computational Linguistics and the 44th annual meeting of the Association for Computational Linguistics*, ACL-44, pages 1–8.

Mohammad Salameh, Colin Cherry, and Grzegorz Kondrak. 2014. Lattice desegmentation for statistical machine translation. In *Proceedings of the 52nd Annual Meeting of the Association for Computational Linguistics (Volume 1: Long Papers)*, pages 100–110.

Kairit Sirts and Sharon Goldwater. 2013. Minimally-supervised morphological segmentation using adaptor grammars. *TACL*, 1:255–266.

David Stallard, Jacob Devlin, Michael Kayser, Yoong Keok Lee, and Regina Barzilay. 2012. Unsupervised morphology rivals supervised morphology for arabic mt. In *Proceedings of the 50th Annual Meeting of the Association for Computational Linguistics: Short Papers - Volume 2*, ACL '12, pages 322–327, Stroudsburg, PA, USA.

Andreas Stolcke. 2002. Srilm - an extensible language modeling toolkit. In *Intl. Conf. Spoken Language Processing*, pages 901–904.

Improving Chinese-English PropBank Alignment

Shumin Wu
Department of Computer Science
University of Colorado Boulder
shumin@colorado.edu

Martha Palmer
Department of Linguistics
University of Colorado Boulder
mpalmer@colorado.edu

Abstract

We describe 2 improvements to Chinese-English PropBank predicate-argument structure alignment. Taking advantage of the recently expanded PropBank English nominal and adjective predicate annotation (Bonial et al., 2014), we performed predicate-argument alignments between both verb and nominal/adjective predicates in Chinese and English. Using our alignment system, this increased the number of aligned predicate-argument structures by 24.5% on the parallel Xinhua News corpus. We also improved the PropBank alignment system using expectation-maximization (EM) techniques. By collecting Chinese-English predicate-to-predicate and argument type-to-argument type alignment probabilities and iteratively improving the alignment output using these probabilities on a large unannotated parallel corpora, we improved the predicate alignment performance by 1 F point when using all automatic SRL and word alignment inputs.

1 Introduction

With the growing interest in building semantically-driven machine translation (MT) systems/evaluation metrics (Carpuat and Wu, 2007; Wu and Fung, 2009b; Wu and Fung, 2009a; Lo and Wu, 2011; Lo et al., 2013; Ma, 2014), the need for a comprehensive and high performing semantic alignment system has become more pressing. While there are finer grained representations such as FrameNet (Baker et al., 1998) and Abstract Meaning Representation (AMR) (Banarescu et al., 2013), PropBank (Palmer et al., 2005) semantic representation has been popular in the MT community partly because of the availability of large quantity of annotated data in multiple languages, enabling the development of accurate automatic semantic role labeling systems.

arg type	Arg0	Arg1	Arg2	Arg3	Arg4	V
Arg0	***1610***	79	25	-	-	9
Arg1	432	***2665***	128	**11**	-	142
Arg2	43	*310*	**140**	8	3	67
Arg3	2	14	*21*	7	-	4
Arg4	1	*37*	9	3	**6**	4
V	25	28	22	1	-	**3278**

Table 1: Chinese argument type (column) to English argument type (row) alignment counts using gold SRL and word alignment annotated Xinhua News data

While the argument types defined in PropBank were intended to be self-contained and independent of the predicate or language, as Fung et al. (2007), Choi et al. (2009), and our previous work (Wu and Palmer, 2011) have demonstrated, assuming alignment between arguments of the same type is insufficient. Table 1 shows the alignment distribution of the core argument types between Chinese and English. While ARG0 and ARG1 alignments are relatively deterministic, alignment involving ARG2-5 and adjunct argument types (not shown) are much more varied. Part of this alignment variety is caused by differences in argument annotation guidelines between English and Chinese, but another part is caused by verb predicates being nominalized in the translation. Our previous work tried to address the first issue by using aligned words in the argument span (instead of the argument type) to align argu-

Proceedings of SSST-9, Ninth Workshop on Syntax, Semantics and Structure in Statistical Translation, pages 74–82,
Denver, Colorado, June 4, 2015. ©2015 Association for Computational Linguistics

ments between English and Chinese. But since we had only considered alignments between verb predicates and their arguments, around 27% of the time, verb predicates are aligned somewhat awkwardly. Another issue we had encountered is, since we solely relied on word alignment input, the approach is not very reliable for aligning short arguments (since a single word alignment error can become critical).

In this work, we attempt to address both of these issues. With the recently expanded PropBank English nominal and adjective predicate annotation (Bonial et al., 2014), we are now able to perform predicate-argument alignments between both verb and nominal/adjective predicates in Chinese and English. With our alignment system, this increased the number of aligned predicate-argument structures by 24.5% on the parallel Xinhua News corpus and allowed more semantically similar predicates to be aligned, regardless of the syntactic form of the predicates. We also propose an extension to our predicate-argument alignment system by factoring in predicate-to-predicate and argument type-to-argument type alignment probabilities when making alignment decisions. Combined with expectation-maximization (EM) techniques that iteratively refines these probabilities, we achieved an 1 F1 point predicate alignment performance improvement using all automatic (SRL and word alignment) inputs. More over, even though the alignment probabilities were generated from automatic system inputs, in some instances, we were able to improve alignment performances using gold SRL inputs.

2 Related Work

Resnik (2004) was one of the earlier works proposing semantic similarity (with a looser definition of semantically similar/equivalent phrases) using triangulation between parallel corpora. This was extended later by Madnani et al. (2008a; 2008b)). Mareček (2009) proposed aligning tectogrammatical trees, where only content (autosemantic) words are nodes, in a parallel English/Czech corpus to improve overall word alignment and thereby improve machine translation. Padó and Lapata (2005; 2006) used word alignment and syntax based argument similarity to project English FrameNet semantic roles to German.

Fung et al. (2007) demonstrated that there is poor semantic parallelism between Chinese-English bilingual sentences. Their technique for improving Chinese-English predicate-argument mapping ($ARG_{Chinese,i} \mapsto ARG_{English,j}$) consists of matching predicates with a bilingual lexicon, computing cosine-similarity (based on lexical translation) of (only) core arguments and tuning on an unannotated parallel corpus. Choi et al. (2009) showed how to enhance Chinese-English verb alignments by exploring predicate-argument structure alignment using parallel PropBanks. The system, using GIZA++ word alignment, deduced alternate verb alignments that showed improvement over pure GIZA++ alignment.

Wu and Fung (2009b) was one of the first to use parallel semantic roles to improve MT system output. Given the outputs from Moses (Koehn et al., 2007), a machine translation decoder, they reordered the translations based on the best predicate-argument alignment. The resulting system showed a 0.5 point BLEU score improvement even though the BLEU metric often discounts improvement in semantic consistency of MT output. To address this issue, Lo and Wu (2011) proposed MEANT, a predicate-argument structure alignment based machine translation evaluation system that better correlates with human MT judgment. Lo et al. (2013) later showed that tuning an MT system against this metric produced more robust translations. Similar ideas on semantically coherent MT have been explored by Ma (2014), where the system attempts to fuse multiple MT translations using predicate-argument alignment metrics, though the results did not show improvement with the BLEU metric.

More recently, Banarescu et al. (2013) have proposed Abstract Meaning Representation (AMR) as an alternative/intermediary representation for MT that may improve the semantic coherency of the output. While the project have only recently gained more traction, an AMR-based MT would likely require aligning AMR concepts between the 2 translation languages. Since AMR is based to a large degree on PropBank SRL, improving SRL alignment should transfer accordingly to improvements in AMR alignments as well.

3 Aligning PropBank Predicate-Arguments

Given a parallel sentence pair, we attempt to find the corresponding PropBank predicate-argument alignments between the sentences as illustrated by figure 1.

3.1 Baseline approach

We first describe our baseline predicate-argument alignment approach (Wu and Palmer, 2011): argument alignments are based on the proportion of aligned words between them, predicate-argument structure alignments are based on the alignment quality of their arguments. We assume there can be a many-to-many argument alignment but only a one-to-one predicate-argument structure alignment between the 2 languages.

Formally, we denote $a_{i,c}$ and $a_{j,e}$ as arguments in Chinese and English respectively, $A_{I,c}$ and $A_{J,e}$ as a set of mapped Chinese and English arguments respectively, $W_{i,c}$ as the words in argument $a_{i,c}$, and $map_e(a_{i,c}) = W_{i,e}$ as the word alignment function that takes the source argument and produces a set of words in the target language sentence. We define precision as the fraction of aligned target words in the mapped argument set:

$$P_{I,c} = \frac{|(\cup_{i \in I} map_e(a_{i,c})) \cap (\cup_{j \in J} W_{j,e})|}{|\cup_{i \in I} map_e(a_{i,c})|} \quad (1)$$

and recall as the fraction of source words in the mapped argument set:

$$R_{I,c} = \frac{\sum_{i \in I} |W_{i,c}|}{\sum_{\forall i} |W_{i,c}|} \quad (2)$$

We then choose the $A_{I,c}$ that optimizes the F1-score of P_c and R_c:

$$A_{I,c} = \arg\max_{I} \frac{2 \cdot P_{I,c} \cdot R_{I,c}}{P_{I,c} + R_{I,c}} = F_{I,c} \quad (3)$$

Finally, to constrain both the source and target argument sets, we optimize:

$$A_{I,c}, A_{J,c} = \arg\max_{I,J} \frac{2 \cdot F_{I,c} \cdot F_{J,e}}{F_{I,c} + F_{J,e}} = F_{IJ} \quad (4)$$

To measure similarity between a single pair of source, target arguments, we define:

$$P_{ij} = \frac{|map_e(a_{i,c}) \cup W_{j,e}|}{|map_e(a_{i,c})|}$$
$$R_{ij} = \frac{|map_c(a_{j,e}) \cup W_{i,c}|}{|map_c(a_{j,e})|} \quad (5)$$

While our work has demonstrated that this approach can produce better predicate alignments than word alignment alone, it can also become confused when there are multiple predicates in a sentence that have shared words in their argument spans, especially when faced with word alignment errors. Figure 2 shows one such example: because the automatic word aligner erroneously aligned both 自筹/*self-provide* and 建设/*construct* to *build* (shown with dotted lines), as well as missed the correct word alignments of 自筹 to *Using its own*, 自筹 is instead aligned to *build*, since they share more aligned words amongst the arguments. However, since the Chinese predicate 建设/*construct* often aligns to *build*, and `ARG1` in Chinese frequently maps to `ARG1` in English but rarely maps to `ARGM-MNR`, an alignment framework that considers these likelihood can potentially correct these types of misalignment.

3.2 Building a alignment probability model

To enhance our baseline approach, we first collect alignment probabilities between a Chinese predicate and its argument types and a English predicate and its argument types. Specifically, we are interested in the following:

$p(pred_{j,e}|pred_{i,c})$: given a Chinese predicate in the mapping, the probability of an English predicate

$p(a_{l,e}|a_{k,c}, pred_{i,c}, pred_{j,e})$: given an aligned Chinese & English predicate pair and the Chinese argument type, the probability of an English argument type

In addition to producing a better alignment output, these 2 probabilities (along with probabilities in the English-to-Chinese alignment direction) may also be used to compute the semantic similarity of a pair of parallel sentences.

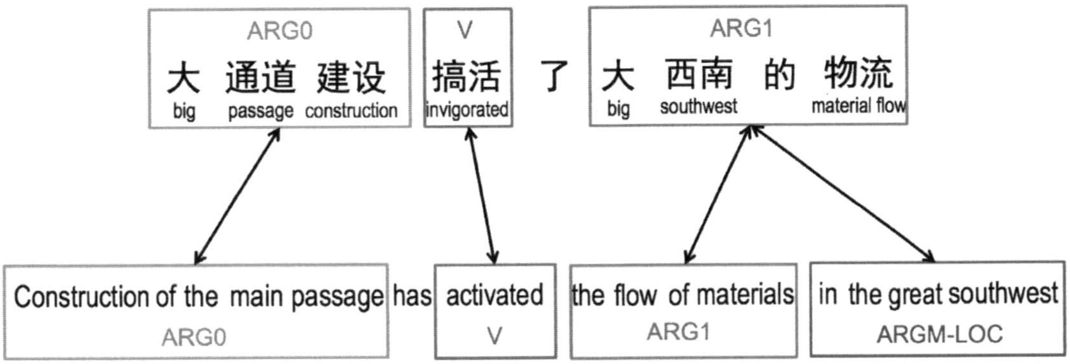

Figure 1: Chinese predicate-arguments mapping example

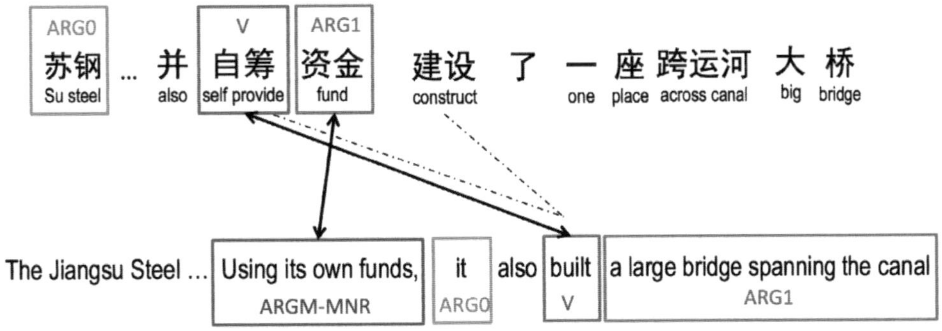

Figure 2: Bad predicate-argument alignment (solid lines) caused by word alignment (dashed lines) error

3.2.1 Predicate-to-predicate mapping probability

There are over 20,000 Chinese predicates and over 10,000 English predicates (in OntoNotes 5.0 PropBank frame files). Even on a large corpora, $freq_{map}(pred_{i,c}, pred_{j,e})$ will be low or zero for many predicate pairs when producing a probability estimate. We chose the Simple Good-Turing smoothing method (Gale, 1995) to smooth the seen mapping frequency counts and estimate the total unseen mapping probability $\sum_{j \in freq_{map}(pred_{i,c}, pred_{j,e})=0} p(pred_{j,e}|pred_{i,c})$.

3.2.2 Argument-to-argument mapping probability

Since $freq_{map}(pred_{j,e}|pred_{i,c})$ is sparse, $freq_{map}(a_{l,e}|pred_{i,c}, pred_{j,e}, a_{k,c})$ will also be sparse. We address this using absolute discounting (Chen and Goodman, 1996) to smooth

$$p(a_{l,e}|a_{k,c}, pred_{i,c}, pred_{j,e}) = \frac{\max(freq(a_{l,e}|a_{k,c}, pred_{i,e}, pred_{j,e}) - d, 0)}{\sum_l freq(a_{l,e}|a_{k,c}, pred_{i,c}, pred_{j,e})} + (1-\lambda) \cdot p_{backoff}(a_{l,e})$$

with a few different back-off probability distributions:

(a) $p(a_{l,e}|a_{k,c}, pred_{i,c})$: given the Chinese predicate and argument type, the probability of an English argument type

(b) $p(a_{l,e}|a_{k,c}, pred_{j,e})$: given the English predicate and Chinese argument type, the probability of an English argument type

(c) $p(a_{l,e}|a_{k,c})$: given the Chinese argument type, the probability of an English argument type

(a) and (b) can be further smoothed using (c), while (c) can be computed directly from the frequency count over a large corpus since there are less than 30 argument types for either Chinese or English. To choose between (a) and (b) as the back-off probability distribution, we compute the *cosine* similarity between (a), (c) and (b), (c) and choose the smaller of the 2 (i.e., choose the more specific distribution that's less similar (more informative) to the base distribution).

3.3 Probabilistic alignment

With the probability model described previously, we attempted to improve predicate-argument alignment by integrating the model with the alignment algorithm. Because the model is computed using automatic system output, we wanted to ensure the alignment algorithm does not overly rely on it. Therefore we modify equation 5 to:

$$\begin{aligned} P'_{kl} &= (1-\beta+\beta\cdot w(a_{l,e}|a_{k,c}, pred_{i,c}, pred_{j,e}))P_{kl} \\ R'_{kl} &= (1-\beta+\beta\cdot w(a_{k,c}|a_{l,e}, pred_{i,c}, pred_{j,e}))R_{kl} \end{aligned} \tag{6}$$

where $0 \leq \beta \leq 1$ and

$$w(a_k) = \frac{p(a_k)}{\sum_k p(a_k)\cdot p(a_k)} \tag{7}$$

so that the expected value of $w(a_k)$, $E(w(a_k)) = 1$. If $P'_{kl} > 1$ or $R'_{kl} > 1$, we change $P'_{kl} = 1$, $R'_{kl} = 1$. We also update equation 3 to take into account predicate-to-predicate mapping likelihood:

$$\begin{aligned} F'_{i,c} &= (1-\alpha+\alpha\cdot w(pred_{j,e}|pred_{i,c}))F_{i,c} \\ F'_{j,e} &= (1-\alpha+\alpha\cdot w(pred_{i,c}|pred_{j,e}))F_{j,e} \end{aligned} \tag{8}$$

We choose α and β (through grid-search) to maximize the sum of the alignment score of all the predicate-argument pairs in the corpus. This is analogous to the maximization step of the expectation–maximization (EM) algorithm. In our case, the expectation step is computing the predicate/argument alignment probabilities.

4 Experiment

4.1 Setup

We used a portion of OntoNotes Release 5.0[1] (with additional nominal/adjective predicates) that has Chinese-English word alignment annotation[2] as the basis for evaluating semantic alignment. This composes around 2000 Xinhua News and 3000 broadcast conversation (CCTV and Phoenix) sentence pairs. Merging the 2 resources result in parallel sentences with gold Treebank, gold PropBank, and gold word alignment annotations, which we dub the triple-gold corpus.

To generate reference predicate-argument alignments, we ran the alignment system with a cutoff threshold of $F_{c,e} < 0.4$ (i.e., alignments with F-score below 0.4 are discarded) using all gold annotations. We selected a small random sample of the Xinhua output and found the output to have both high precision and recall, with only occasional discrepancies caused by possible word alignment errors (and was no worse than inter-annotator disagreements). For predicate-argument alignments using automatic word alignment input, we chose a cutoff threshold of $F_{c,e} < 0.2$.

We trained our Chinese SRL system (Wu and Palmer, 2015) with Berkeley Parser output on Chinese PropBank 1.0 (all Xinhua News, excluding files in the triple-gold corpus). We trained our English SRL system (same architecture as the Chinese SRL system) with Berkley parser output on OntoNotes Release 5.0 (excluding files in the triple-gold corpus) and BOLT phase 1 data (which also includes nominal annotation). We use the Berkeley aligner trained on a 1.6M sentence parallel corpora collected from a variety of sources[3]. These same corpora were also used to build our probabilistic alignment model.

4.2 Alignment with Nominal/Adjective Predicates

We evaluated the impact of alignment with the addition of non-verb predicates on Xinhua News, as the broadcast conversation sections lack Chinese nominal annotations. In table 3, we restrict alignments to between only verb predicates, verb predicates with the addition of Chinese nominal predicates, and

[1]LDC2013T19

[2]LDC2009E83

[3]LDC2002E18, LDC2002L27, LDC2003E07, LDC2003E14, LDC2004T08, LDC2005E83, LDC2005T06, LDC2005T10, LDC2005T34, LDC2006E24, LDC2006E26, LDC2006E34, LDC2006E85, LDC2006E86, LDC2006E92, LDC2006E93

pred. type	V_c-V_e	N_c-V_e	V_c-N_e	N_c-N_e	total
verb only	4879	-	-	-	4879
+Ch. nom.	4762	274	-	-	5036
+En. nom.	4849	-	384	-	5233
all pred.	4759	239	314	760	6072

Table 2: Predicate-argument mapping counts on Xinhua News, where only verb predicate annotations were available or verb and nominal/adjective predicate annotations. V_c represents Chinese verb predicates, N_e represents English nominal/adjective predicates

verb predicates with the addition of English nominal/adjective predicates, as well as allowing all predicate types.

The results show that the addition of nominal and adjective predicates for both English and Chinese increased the overall number of aligned Chinese and English predicate-argument structures by 24.5%. While a large portion of the additional alignments are of the non-verb to non-verb types, the availability of the non-verb predicates also allowed some previously unaligned verb predicates to align to non-verb predicates. This increased the total number of aligned Chinese verb predicates by 4.0% and aligned English verb predicates by 2.4%. Also, some verb predicates that were previously forced to align to another verb predicate have now found a more semantically similar non-verb predicate (evident by the decreased overall number of verb-to-verb alignments).

4.3 Alignment Probability Model

We produced the alignment probability model using the 1.6M sentence pair corpus, The EM algorithm converged after 2-3 iterations, as the alignments did not vary wildly with different α and β values (optimal $\alpha = 0.15$, $\beta = 0.1$). In general, the choice of β had a smaller impact on the overall mapping score of the corpus than α.

The results, detailed in table 3, show that using automatic SRL and word alignment, the probability model improved semantic alignment by about 1 F point on both Xinhua News (includes non-verb predicates) and broadcast conversation (verb predicates only for Chinese) sections. These improvements were found to be statistically significant[4] ($p \leq 0.01$). Surprisingly, the probability model (which was extracted from automatic SRL output), was able to improve the performance of the system using gold standard SRL input by 0.78 F point on broadcast conversation (also statistically significant w/ $p \leq 0.01$). For Xinhua News, the already very high baseline (92.40 F1) likely prevented any additional improvements.

With gold word alignment input, however, the probability model was not able to improve the results of either corpus section, even though the performances are lower than when using gold SRL inputs. This is not surprising as the probability model can suggest more semantically coherent alignments when faced with word alignment errors, but does not actually correct any input SRL mistakes made by automatic systems.

We also experimented with building the probability model using only 10% of the data. The improvements were generally 0.1-0.3 F points less than using the full dataset. The optimal $\alpha = 0.15$ and $\beta = 0.1$ did not change.

Inspecting the output, we found the probabilistic alignment system was able to correct the bad alignment example in figure 2 (corrected in figure 3), as the aligner preferred the more probable `ARG1` to `ARG1` alignment between 自筹 and *use* instead of the less probable `ARG1` to `ARGM-MNR` alignment between 自筹 and *build*. This also allowed the correct alignment between 建设/*construct* and *build* (also boosted by the increased predicate-to-predicate alignment probability).

While the predicate alignment performance difference between using automatic SRL and gold standard SRL input is around 7 F points, there is a much larger gap in core argument alignment performance: on Xinhua News, automatic SRL based output produced a 73.83 F-score While this is comparable to Fung et al. (Fung et al., 2007)'s 72.5 (albeit with different sections of the corpus and based on gold standard predicates from a bi-lingual dictionary), it's 18.27 F points lower than using gold standard SRL based output. When including all arguments, automatic SRL based output achieved 69.14% while the gold SRL based output achieved 87.56%. The performance on broadcast conversation shows a similar

[4] *SIGF* (www.nlpado.de/%7esebastian/software/sigf.shtml), using stratified approximate randomization test (Yeh, 2000)

corpus	system	predicate pair			core argument label			all argument label		
		p	r	f1	p	r	f1	p	r	f1
Xinhua News	baseline	86.93	82.56	84.69	80.27	67.04	73.06	75.14	62.53	68.26
	+prob model	87.97	83.47	**85.66**	81.07	67.78	**73.83**	76.64	62.98	**69.14**
	gold SRL	93.67	91.16	92.40	94.45	89.93	92.13	90.71	84.63	87.56
	+prob model	93.02	90.38	91.68	93.91	89.54	91.67	90.62	83.26	86.78
	gold WA	90.83	87.42	89.09	83.16	71.55	76.92	80.42	71.11	75.48
	+prob model	91.21	87.45	89.29	83.48	71.57	77.07	80.84	70.64	75.40
broadcast conversation	baseline	80.45	78.50	79.46	72.87	57.77	64.45	64.88	51.89	57.66
	+prob model	81.52	79.51	**80.50**	73.75	58.40	**65.18**	66.28	52.27	**58.45**
	gold SRL	89.50	85.29	87.34	90.21	82.19	86.02	82.61	75.20	78.73
	+prob model	90.17	86.15	**88.12**	90.82	82.93	**86.70**	84.11	75.25	**79.43**
	gold WA	87.02	86.66	86.84	78.31	65.11	71.10	74.85	64.94	69.55
	+prob model	87.17	86.61	86.89	78.26	64.80	70.89	74.96	64.20	69.16

Table 3: Predicate-argument mapping improvements using the probability model

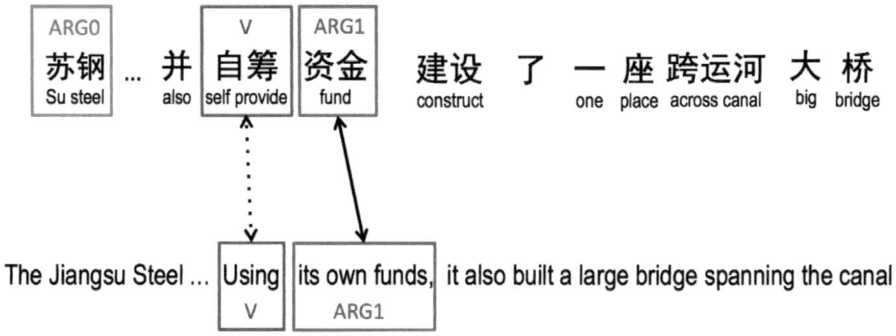

Figure 3: Corrected alignment using the probability model

drop between the 2 SRL outputs. Still, the probability model was able to generate statistically significant improvements to argument alignments when using automatic SRL inputs, albeit with a smaller margin.

These argument results are not too surprising given the alignment system need to deal with many sources of error, from errors introduced by the automatic Chinese SRL, English SRL and word alignment systems to incompatibilities between English and Chinese frame files, as well as confusions arising from implicit arguments. Along with the lack of improvement in predicate alignment performance when the probability alignment model uses gold word alignment input, the results indicate that a higher-performing PropBank alignment system need to address automatic SRL errors.

5 Conclusion

We described 2 improvements to Chinese-English PropBank alignments. The first takes advantage of expanded English nominal/adjective predicate annotation to produce a more comprehensive PropBank alignment between Chinese and English, increasing the number of aligned Chinese and English predicate-argument structures by 24.5%. The second utilizes predicate-argument alignment probabilities extracted from a large unannotated parallel corpus to both improve predicate-argument alignment performance and provide a probability model that can be used to evaluate/improve semantically-driven machine translation.

Given that the probability model, built using all automatic system output, provides smaller improvements to (or even degrades) the system when either gold standard SRL or word alignment is used, it still has room for improvement. One such possible improvement would be to build a probability model predicated on verb classes/clusters. This could address the sparse alignment frequency count issue from the many possible Chinese-English predicate-argument pairings. For English, we can use the existing VerbNet class resource and train an automatic system for polysemous verbs. For Chinese, however, we would need to either induce verb classes through mapping (Wu et al., 2010), or via an automatic verb clustering method.

While we have achieved good predicate-argument alignment performance, specific argument alignment performance still lags behind. One reason is that while we can induce correct predicate-argument mapping from the argument mapping pairs, even when the predicates themselves are misaligned, for argument alignment, our system currently does not attempt to directly correct argument labels from automatic SRL output. Therefore, any SRL labeling error in the automatic SRL system output (made worse by having 2 languages) is propagated through the alignment system. A joint-inference/joint-learning framework between semantic alignment, SRL (including joint inference of Chinese and English SRL as proposed by Zhuang and Zong (2010)), and word alignment could potentially address the shortcomings in our current implementation.

Acknowledgement

We gratefully acknowledge the support of the National Science Foundation CISE-IISRI-0910992, Richer Representations for Machine Translation and, DARPA FA8750-09-C-0179 (via BBN) Machine Reading: Ontology Induction: Semlink+. Any opinions, findings, and conclusions or recommendations expressed in this material are those of the authors and do not necessarily reflect the views of the National Science Foundation.

References

Collin F. Baker, Charles J. Fillmore, and John B. Lowe. 1998. The berkeley framenet project. In *Proceedings of the 36th Annual Meeting of the Association for Computational Linguistics and 17th International Conference on Computational Linguistics - Volume 1*, ACL '98, pages 86–90, Stroudsburg, PA, USA. Association for Computational Linguistics.

Laura Banarescu, Claire Bonial, Shu Cai, Madalina Georgescu, Kira Griffitt, Ulf Hermjakob, Kevin Knight, Philipp Koehn, Martha Palmer, and Nathan Schneider. 2013. Abstract meaning representation for sembanking. In *Proceedings of the 7th Linguistic Annotation Workshop and Interoperability with Discourse*, pages 178–186, Sofia, Bulgaria, August. Association for Computational Linguistics.

Claire Bonial, Julia Bonn, Kathryn Conger, Jena D. Hwang, and Martha Palmer. 2014. Propbank: Semantics of new predicate types. In *Proceedings of the Ninth International Conference on Language Resources and Evaluation (LREC'14)*, Reykjavik, Iceland, may.

Marine Carpuat and Dekai Wu. 2007. Improving statistical machine translation using word sense disambiguation. In *The 2007 Joint Conference on Empirical Methods in Natural Language Processing and Computational Natural Language Learning (EMNLP-CoNLL 2007)*, pages 61–72.

Stanley F. Chen and Joshua Goodman. 1996. An empirical study of smoothing techniques for language modeling. In *Proceedings of the 34th Annual Meeting on Association for Computational Linguistics*, ACL '96, pages 310–318, Stroudsburg, PA, USA. Association for Computational Linguistics.

Jinho D. Choi, Martha Palmer, and Nianwen Xue. 2009. Using parallel propbanks to enhance word-alignments. In *Proceedings of ACL-IJCNLP workshop on Linguistic Annotation (LAW'09)*, pages 121–124.

Pascale Fung, Zhaojun Wu, Yongsheng Yang, and Dekai Wu. 2007. Learning bilingual semantic frames: Shallow semantic parsing vs. semantic role projection. In *11th Conference on Theoretical and Methodological Issues in Machine Translation*, pages 75–84.

William A. Gale. 1995. Good-turing smoothing without tears. *Journal of Quantitative Linguistics*, 2.

Philipp Koehn, Hieu Hoang, Alexandra Birch, Chris Callison-Burch, Marcello Federico, Nicola Bertoldi, Brooke Cowan, Wade Shen, Christine Moran, Richard Zens, Chris Dyer, Ondrej Bojar, Alexandra Constantin, and Evan Herbst. 2007. Moses: Open source toolkit for statistical machine translation. In *Proceedings of the Annual Meeting of the Association for Computational Linguistics (ACL'07), demonstration session*, pages 177–180.

Chi-kiu Lo and Dekai Wu. 2011. Meant: An inexpensive, high-accuracy, semi-automatic metric for evaluating translation utility via semantic frames. In *In Proceedings of 49th Annual Meeting of the Association for Computational Linguistics: Human Language Technologies (ACL HLT 2011)*.

Chi-kiu Lo, Karteek Addanki, Markus Saers, and Dekai Wu. 2013. Improving machine translation by training against an automatic semantic frame based evaluation metric. In *In Proceedings of 51th Annual Meeting of the Association for Computational Linguistics: Human Language Technologies (ACL HLT 2013)*.

Wei-Yun Ma. 2014. *Hybrid System Combination for Machine Translation: An Integration of Phrase-level and Sentences-level Combination Approaches*. Ph.D. thesis, Columbia University.

Nitin Madnani, Philip Resnik, Bonnie Dorr, and Richard Schwartz. 2008a. Applying automatically generated semantic knowledge: A case study in machine translation. In *NSF Symposium on Semantic Knowledge Discovery, Organization and Use*.

Nitin Madnani, Philip Resnik, Bonnie Dorr, and Richard Schwartz. 2008b. Are multiple reference translations necessary? investigating the value of paraphrased reference translations in parameter optimization. In *Proceedings of the 8th Conference of the Association for Machine Translation in the Americas (AMTA'08)*.

David Mareček. 2009. Using tectogrammatical alignment in phrase-based machine translation. In *Proceedings of WDS 2009 Contributed Papers*, pages 22—27.

Sebastian Padó and Mirella Lapata. 2005. Cross-linguistic projection of role-semantic information. In *Proceedings of the conference on Human Language Technology and Empirical Methods in Natural Language Processing*, HLT '05, pages 859–866, Stroudsburg, PA, USA. Association for Computational Linguistics.

Sebastian Padó and Mirella Lapata. 2006. Optimal constituent alignment with edge covers for semantic projection. In *Proceedings of the 21st International Conference on Computational Linguistics and the 44th annual meeting of the Association for Computational Linguistics*, ACL-44, pages 1161–1168, Stroudsburg, PA, USA. Association for Computational Linguistics.

Martha Palmer, Daniel Gildea, and Paul Kingsbury. 2005. The proposition bank: An annotated corpus of semantic roles. *Computational Linguistics*, pages 71–106.

Philip Resnik. 2004. Exploiting hidden meanings: Using bilingual text for monolingual annotation. In Alexander Gelbukh, editor, *Lecture Notes in Computer Science 2945: Computational Linguistics and Intelligent Text Processing*, pages 283–299. Springer.

Dekai Wu and Pascale Fung. 2009a. Can semantic role labeling improve smt? In *Proceedings of the 13th Annual Conference of the EAMT*, pages 218–225, Barcelona, Spain.

Dekai Wu and Pascale Fung. 2009b. Semantic roles for smt: A hybrid two-pass model. In *Proceedings of the North American Chapter of the Association for Computational Linguistics - Human Language Technologies (NAACL-HLT'09)*, pages 13–16.

Shumin Wu and Martha Palmer. 2011. Semantic mapping using automatic word alignment and semantic role labeling. In *Proceedings of ACL-HLT workshop on Syntax, Semantics and Structure in Statistical Translation (SSST-5)*.

Shumin Wu and Martha Palmer. 2015. Can selectional preference help automatic semantic role labeling? In *Proceedings of the 4th Joint Conference on Lexical and Computational Semantics (⋆SEM)*.

Shumin Wu, Jinho D. Choi, and Martha Palmer. 2010. Detecting cross-lingual semantic similarity using parallel propbanks. In *Proceedings of the 9th Conference of the Association for Machine Translation in the Americas*.

Alexander Yeh. 2000. More accurate tests for the statistical significance of result differences. In *Proceedings of the 18th Conference on Computational Linguistics - Volume 2*, COLING '00, pages 947–953, Stroudsburg, PA, USA. Association for Computational Linguistics.

Tao Zhuang and Chengqing Zong. 2010. Joint inference for bilingual semantic role labeling. In *Proceedings of EMNLP 2010*, pages 304–314, Cambridge, MA, October. Association for Computational Linguistics.

Author Index